THE LAYMAN'S BIBLE COMMENTARY

THE LAYMAN'S BIBLE COMMENTARY
IN TWENTY-FIVE VOLUMES

THE LAYMAN'S
BIBLE COMMENTARY

Balmer H. Kelly, *Editor*

Donald G. Miller   *Associate Editors*   Arnold B. Rhodes

Dwight M. Chalmers, *Editor,* John Knox Press

VOLUME 17

THE GOSPEL ACCORDING TO

MARK

Paul S. Minear

JOHN KNOX PRESS

ATLANTA, GEORGIA

© M. E. Bratcher 1962

10 9 8 7 6 5 4 3 2

Complete set: ISBN: 0-8042-3086-2
This volume: 0-8042-3077-3
Library of Congress Card Number: 59-10454
First paperback edition 1982
Printed in the United States of America
John Knox Press
Atlanta, Georgia 30365

PREFACE

The LAYMAN'S BIBLE COMMENTARY is based on the conviction that the Bible has the Word of good news for the whole world. The Bible is not the property of a special group. It is not even the property and concern of the Church alone. It is given to the Church for its own life but also to bring God's offer of life to all mankind—wherever there are ears to hear and hearts to respond.

It is this point of view which binds the separate parts of the LAYMAN'S BIBLE COMMENTARY into a unity. There are many volumes and many writers, coming from varied backgrounds, as is the case with the Bible itself. But also as with the Bible there is a unity of purpose and of faith. The purpose is to clarify the situations and language of the Bible that it may be more and more fully understood. The faith is that in the Bible there is essentially one Word, one message of salvation, one gospel.

The LAYMAN'S BIBLE COMMENTARY is designed to be a concise non-technical guide for the layman in personal study of his own Bible. Therefore, no biblical text is printed along with the comment upon it. This commentary will have done its work precisely to the degree in which it moves its readers to take up the Bible for themselves.

The writers have used the Revised Standard Version of the Bible as their basic text. Occasionally they have differed from this translation. Where this is the case they have given their reasons. In the main, no attempt has been made either to justify the wording of the Revised Standard Version or to compare it with other translations.

One objective in this commentary is to provide the most helpful explanation of fundamental matters in simple up-to-date terms. Exhaustive treatment of subjects has not been undertaken.

In our age knowledge of the Bible is perilously low. At the same time there are signs that many people are longing for help in getting such knowledge. Knowledge of and about the Bible is, of course, not enough. The grace of God and the work of the Holy Spirit are essential to the renewal of life through the Scriptures. It is in the happy confidence that the great hunger for the Word is a sign of God's grace already operating within men, and that the Spirit works most wonderfully where the Word is familiarly known, that this commentary has been written and published.

THE EDITORS AND
THE PUBLISHERS

THE GOSPEL ACCORDING TO

MARK

INTRODUCTION

The Churches in Rome

The book we know as the Gospel according to Mark was in all likelihood written in the city of Rome during the middle decades of the first century A.D. We may well begin our study, therefore, by trying to picture that city. Situated in Italy, on both sides of the Tiber River, the ancient city occupied roughly the same location as does today's Rome. Its population was probably well over a million and included people who had migrated from all provinces of the empire and even from beyond its frontiers. Jostling each other on its streets were men of many nations. Some had been drawn by the magnetic pull of commerce; others had been brought as slaves from territories conquered by Roman legions. They had brought with them their own cults and cultures, their ancestral traditions and tongues. In the shops, therefore, virtually all the languages of the Mediterranean world could be heard, although, as in most polyglot cities, the people of a given tongue and heritage gravitated toward the same borough of the city.

Rome was the administrative headquarters for a powerful empire, reaching from Spain in the west to unruly Parthia in the east, from Britain in the north to the land of the Egyptians and the Carthaginians in the south. From its extensive barracks, legions of soldiers were dispatched to keep order within a vast domain and to extend the boundary of political power. This was the city of emperors, the site of palaces, of senate buildings, of courts and temples, a city even more impressive then than it is today—the queen of the world.

Rome was also the undisputed financial and commercial center of the empire. It was linked closely to all parts of the empire by land and sea routes, by frequent courier service, and by a surprising volume of travel and trade. All roads did in fact lead to—and away from—Rome. On the success of ocean-borne trade its people were dependent for both their necessities and their luxuries (see Rev. 18:11-13 for a sample list). The value of the currency was basically controlled by its banks and legislators, so that Romans (or at least some of them) would profit from successive waves of inflation or deflation. Here was determined the amount of taxes to be collected from the provinces; here were levied all sorts of duties—excise, import, and export—on the flow of trade. As was true of earlier and later Babylons, Rome embodied the grandeur and shame, the wealth and poverty, the power and cruelty, the administrative efficiency and petty bureaucracy, of human society at its worst and at its best.

The student who is interested in what happened in this ancient city must perforce follow a calendar which is punctuated by the accessions of successive emperors. Four of these are significant during the first generation of Christian history:

(1) Tiberius (A.D. 14-37), the sovereign during Jesus' ministry (Luke 3:1) and the one who appointed the governors of Judea;

(2) Caligula (A.D. 37-41), called "the mad emperor," whose orders to install his ensign in the Jerusalem Temple provoked riots among the Jews;

(3) Claudius (A.D. 41-54), who expelled many Jews from Rome after the introduction of the Christian movement had excited disturbances among them (Acts 18:2);

(4) Nero (A.D. 54-68), an erratic and turbulent ruler, whose career ended in suicide after his repudiation by the Senate.

Although the enthronement of these rulers punctuated the calendar, and although their policies affected the fortunes of all groups, including the Christians, the Christian movement established more direct contact with the lowlier folk and became more deeply rooted among groups which were far less powerful and prominent (I Cor. 1:26-29). In Rome, as elsewhere, the first community to feel the impact of the Christian gospel was the house of Israel. Already more sons of this house lived outside Palestine than within it. Because of faithfulness to the Covenant with their God, many of them remained strangers and aliens, refusing assimilation into pagan citizenries. For the same reason Gentile hostility toward them remained, and slight provocations could produce bloody anti-Semitic riots in almost every city at any time. Not all Jews, to be sure, obeyed the command to remain separate. Then, as now, it must have seemed the path of prudence to become wholly identified with the holders of power. Yet the synagogues persisted, and to Roman citizens they must often have appeared as centers of sedition and treason.

Certainly this was the case in Rome, where Jews formed one of the largest of the foreign blocs. They had lived in this city for over a century, ever since Pompey had brought slaves and hostages from his capture of Jerusalem in 63 B.C. During subsequent decades other Jews had come voluntarily, drawn by business affiliations and opportunities. By the time of the Christian invasion of Rome, the Jewish community probably numbered more than fifty thousand: slaves, manual laborers, traders, shopkeepers, professional people. Their shops and homes were clustered together in various wards of the city.

Near their homes they established synagogues, of which the names of thirteen have been recovered by historians. Attached to each synagogue was a school for both children and adults. Here the Scriptures were systematically studied, and here on the Sabbath they were publicly read and expounded as an essential act of worship. Here the holy days of Israel, the festivals and the fasts, were faithfully celebrated. Some of the Roman neighbors of the Jews, attracted to their ancient and austere faith, probably attended the synagogues and became familiar with their traditions and hopes. But others were repelled and became suspicious of these foreigners with their strange customs and their staunch loyalty to an alien god. And among the Jews themselves controversy was continuous—between those who loved and those who detested Rome, between those who favored and those who feared assimilation, between those whose hearts were still fixed on the Judean homeland and those who had fused their hopes on achieving greater wealth and status in the western metropolis.

Into this vortex of world power, and into this cluster of synagogues, came messengers from Judea bearing the announcement that the God of Israel had now at long last sent a deliverer to his people and that this deliverer had been crucified in the Holy City. We will never know exactly what brought them, whether they came on business, or on visits to kinfolk, or at the command of employers, or simply from the constraint to bring the news of deliverance. We can do little more than speculate concerning the earliest days of the Christians in Rome. A few clues, however, may be recovered from surviving records.

The first episode in the life of the Roman churches which left traces in written history came during the reign of Claudius (A.D. 41-54). These traces were the direct result of trouble aroused by the Christians, trouble so pronounced as to call for their expulsion from Rome. According to Acts 18:1-3, when Paul first reached Corinth, he found a place to live and to work with Aquila and Priscilla (about A.D. 50). It is almost certain that this couple were Christian Jews who had themselves been active in mission work in Rome. They had lately moved from Italy to Corinth because "Claudius had commanded all the Jews to leave Rome." This casual remark in Acts is corroborated by the Roman historian Suetonius, who told his readers that Claudius had expelled certain Jews from Rome because a certain "Chrestos" had instigated riots among them. Putting these two clues together and drawing the likely inferences, we may conclude that Aquila and his wife had probably provoked those disorders through their efforts to convince other Jews in the Roman synagogues that Jesus of Nazareth was in fact God's Messiah (*Christos*). Whether or not Aquila and his wife were the first to bring the news of Jesus to Rome we do not know, but we do know that the news, when it came to Rome, soon set off an explosion among the synagogues. The reports of riots under Claudius suggest that those who believed in Jesus as God's Messiah were willing, for his sake, to accept sharp resistance from their neighbors and kinsmen. We will come back to this point after noticing the second bit of evidence concerning the Roman churches, this clue being provided, only a few years after Claudius' edict, by Paul's letter to the Christians in Rome.

It is altogether probable that, even as early as Claudius' edict, there had been more than one congregation in Rome. A handful of disciples would hardly have caused such a riot as to require the emperor's sweeping effort to expel all the troublemakers. This supposition is strengthened by the postscript to Paul's letter (Rom. 16), which probably, although not certainly, was included in Paul's original letter. In this postscript Paul wrote as if he knew of the existence of several

Christian cells in the capital city. He spoke of the church which gathered in the home of Aquila and Priscilla (Rom. 16:5). Another congregation seems to have met regularly in the house of Aristobulus (Rom. 16:10), another in the house of Narcissus (Rom. 16:11), another in the house of Asyncritus (Rom. 16:14), and still another in the house of Philologus (Rom. 16:15). Other house-churches may have been represented by the other disciples whom he mentions. All in all, he greeted more than five congregations and more than twenty-five individuals. What an impressive list of church members in Rome! How much we would know if we knew their whole story! Yet we know little more than their names. There must have been many other staunch believers whose names have been wholly lost.

One thing is overwhelmingly clear from this list: Claudius, the emperor, had failed. Within a very short time after his efforts to expel the believers, there had developed at least five house-congregations of whose existence Paul had learned in distant Corinth. These congregations were scattered in different sections of the huge metropolis on the Tiber. Some were Jewish in membership, some Gentile, some mixed. Some were led by men who had been followers of Christ for as long as twenty years. The leaders in some were women, of whom Paul salutes at least six. These groups were, in all likelihood, not well known to one another. The city was large. There was no page for church announcements in the daily paper. There was no separate building for church assemblies, no headquarters, no staff. Yet the various house-churches maintained some contact with fellow believers in other provinces, in Judea, Achaia, and Asia. Travelers moved constantly from one congregation in the East to another in Rome. In fact, one of Paul's reasons for writing was to introduce the deaconess from the household of faith in Cenchreae, who doubtless intended to continue her ministry after moving to Rome (Rom. 16:1-2).

Paul's letter to the Roman congregations tells us far more, however, than simply the names of Roman Christians and the number of houses in which they met. It provides valuable clues concerning what was going on in those congregations, what difficulties they were facing. Because this letter preceded Mark's work in Rome by less than a decade, we should pay heed to these clues.

Paul's discussion in Romans 14 and 15 shows all too clearly that these churches were at odds with one another. House-churches composed of Jews did not extend hospitality to Gentile Christians. Why not? Because these Gentile brothers refused to consider the Sabbath Day holy, according to the commandment of the Law (Deut. 5:12). Furthermore, they refused to observe the dietary commandments of the Law, but were in the habit of eating any food, however unclean it might be judged by Scripture. Jewish Christians were therefore impelled by loyalty to God's Word to consider Gentile Christians unclean and to refuse to eat with them. From the opposite side, these Gentile Christians quite naturally despised and ridiculed their Jewish brothers who held such compunctions about what days were holy and what foods clean. They tried to persuade Jewish disciples to break the Law even before their consciences would permit them to do so. So whenever the two groups met, they fell to wrangling about food and holy days. Their animosities destroyed the peace and joy which should have been theirs in the Holy Spirit (Rom. 14:17).

The issue was far more serious than twentieth-century Gentiles can easily imagine. Far more was involved than "blue laws" and dietary fads. What was involved may become clearer to us if we consider the series of questions which Paul poses in his letter to Jews and Gentiles in Rome. Each question reflects a heated debate among those readers, a debate in which both negative and positive answers were firmly held, a debate which steadily increased division within the churches.

Consider, for example, the question: "What advantage has the Jew?" (Rom. 3:1). This query was the occasion for endless friction among the Roman Christians. Some answered, "None"; others answered, "Great advantage, indeed." And these two groups could hardly live in peace with each other. As another example, "Has God rejected his people?"—that is, Israel (Rom. 11:1). Again we infer that there were Roman Christians who rejoiced in the affirmation (anti-Semitism is not a modern invention) and others who insisted on the negation. The debate was a warm one, as it always is when some groups are being excluded from the select circle or given inferior positions.

These questions may be sufficient to illustrate how deep and difficult were the chasms between one group of Roman believers and another. The student of Mark should carefully examine the other key queries in Paul's letter to the Romans. Many of them sprang from the controversies over the continuing validity of the Law and the Prophets. "What then shall we say about Abraham . . .?" Did not God promise a unique destiny to his descendants? (Rom. 4:1). Does circumcision lose its value in this new day? (Rom. 2:25). Does faith in Jesus Christ justify us in overthrowing the Law? (Rom. 3:31). If we ignore God's demand for obedience to his will, as embodied in Moses' covenant, will faith in the gospel alone be adequate to ensure salvation? (Rom. 1:16). If so, does this mean that the more we sin, the more we honor the power of grace? (Rom. 6:1). All these questions reveal agonizing hostilities within the churches, and poignant need for reconciliation.

Paul's letter thus echoes the dilemmas of the Roman believers. But it also suggests that these believers were bound together by forces of which they were only partly aware. If we are to understand the churches for whom Mark's Gospel was written, we must ask not only about the tensions within their fellowship but also about the forces which held them together. The Apostle who had heard so much about their disputes knew something as well about these cohesive forces.

All of them had heard God's summons to believe in the good news and had accepted it. All had been loved by God, had been claimed as his property by Christ. All shared the same status as Christ's slaves. All were therefore saints (Rom. 1:1-7). Having accepted the same gospel, they had received redemption as a gift (Rom. 3:24) which God had offered to them while they were his enemies (Rom. 5:10). They thus shared in the same status before God, however different might be their standing within the political, economic, or religious brackets of Roman society. In fact, Paul reminds them that every one of them has already passed through death. They are now "dead men on holiday," living on time borrowed, or rather given to them, from God. Together they had died with Christ, and had been united to him in the hope of "a resurrection like his" (Rom. 6:1-11). Henceforth this Master was their owner. Everything given to them was given by him, therefore their first obligation was to give thanks to him. So complete was his control over them that such matters as whether they died or continued to live did not affect their destiny. Even so decisive a matter as death had lost its power to separate them from him. How much less power, then, should be assigned to those matters on which they were at odds. For those who had inherited God's Kingdom, such things as earthly wealth or social status or religious practice could no longer serve as barriers to hospitality. Such was the logic of faith as Paul understood it.

This, then, is a brief sketch of conditions in the Roman churches a decade or so before Mark, and we need not suppose that conditions had greatly changed when his Gospel was written. Judging by these two glimpses into the story of the Roman churches (the edict of Claudius and the letter of Paul) we may infer that certain factors remained rather constant. First of all, there is evidence of sharp conflicts between Christians and the Roman authorities. Claudius had driven out Priscilla, Aquila, and others. Paul speaks of the perils of persecution as normal results of discipleship (Rom. 8:35-36). No society of that day welcomed the appearance of the Church. Second, this opposition of the political authorities was often occasioned by quarrels between the synagogues and the congregations of believers, as well as between Jewish Christians and Gentile Christians. These quarrels usually were provoked by the fact that to some Christians faith required loyalty to the sacred Scriptures while to others it required their rejection. Third, when this conflict developed among believers, those who minimized the clash between the gospel and the Law were usually those who wanted to allay the hostility of synagogue leaders and the suspicions of the state. On the other hand, those whose faith in the gospel produced maximum freedom from the Law found themselves accentuating the hostility of both Jewish and Roman leaders.

These matters were still disturbing the Roman community a few years later when Paul himself came to Rome as a prisoner. For glimpses of this situation, we may well turn to his letter to the Philippian church, written, as most interpreters conclude, from a prison in Rome. Paul was not alarmed or angered by imprisonment. He did not worry about the outcome of his trial even though it might result in his execution. Because it was his work for Christ which had led to jail, he was confident that Christ's work would be advanced by his imprisonment, whether or not it ended in the death penalty (Phil. 1:12-26). It seemed to him entirely reasonable that those who served a crucified Messiah should be ready to share his cross. Jail was the ideal place for announcing a gospel which freed men from all anxieties. The letter also makes clear how completely Paul the Jew (and he remained Jew to the end) had been freed by the gospel from counting as gain any privilege or status accruing from his heritage, his achievement, or his piety (Phil. 3:1-16).

But our chief interest here is not in Paul but in the Roman churches. What effects did Paul's presence have upon them? He himself tells us of the two major reactions, neither of which should be surprising to us. We may call these responses that of the "care-free" and that of the "care-full." The care-free had welcomed Paul's arrival in Rome as a convict. They had taken the risk of visiting him, thus admitting that if he were guilty of sedition they were as well. Like him, they were confident that the living Christ could use even the scandal of a death sentence to advance his cause. Paul's example made them bolder than ever to preach in the streets the same chain-breaking gospel, although this invited similar arrest and chains. They were thus freed from the care to placate Jewish and Roman authorities.

But the care-free disciples enhanced the anxieties of the care-full. Responsible leaders, these men sincerely felt that greater caution was necessary to prevent bloodshed and even the extermination of the Church. They felt that Paul's fate discredited *his* message and *his* way of preaching it. Believers could not hope to succeed if they flouted both the standards of God's Law and the requirements of peace with the empire. To Paul, these care-full saints were "enemies of the cross of Christ" because they did not really accept that cross as demanding of them a like humility, a like obedience, a like freedom (Phil. 1:15-17; 3:18-19). To them, Paul endangered everything with his radical and uncompromising attack upon all securities, all superiorities, all cautions.

Can any guess be more certain than that these two groups must have found it hard to live together within the same brotherhood? Paul's presence in prison, and his bold advice from that pulpit, must have prompted heated debate at every meeting. We can readily imagine some of the epithets which would cut through the air: "dogs" is one of the milder ones (Phil. 3:2). Behind the debates would lie the same issue: "Assuming that we confess Jesus as the Messiah, to what extent does this faith demand from us a message like Paul's, a way of life which breaks all the rules of the Law, participation in a breach of the peace which may lead to prison and death?"

So the story of the Roman churches takes shape, a story which Mark would have heard and which his readers would have remembered. When the Christian message had first appeared (perhaps thirty years earlier), it had created such hostility among both Jews and Gentiles that its exponents were attacked by the former and expelled by the latter. Later (perhaps twenty years earlier than Mark), Paul's letter to the Christians had reflected continuing strife not only with the political rulers (Rom. 13:1-7) and the synagogues, but also among the Christians themselves. Still later (perhaps ten years before Mark), when the same Apostle had written to the church in Philippi from a Roman prison, he had disclosed the same violent conflicts: with Roman authorities, for he was still in jail; with the synagogues, for he was still accused of destroying the Scriptures; and with other Christian leaders, for Paul charged them with envy and jealousy, with cowardice and anxious compromises, with unwillingness to carry the cross.

The whole confused situation reached explosive intensity very soon after Paul wrote to Philippi. In that letter Paul had mentioned the possibility of his execution, but had expressed the conviction that he would be released (1:20-26). What happened was something quite different. With many other Christians he was made the scapegoat of a great disaster which befell the city on July 19, A.D. 63. Curiously enough, this disaster is not mentioned in the New Testament but only in the secular histories of the period. A fire broke out in the shops in a crowded central section of Rome. Fanned by strong winds it swept fiercely through the narrow passages and congested streets, killing hundreds and perhaps thousands of the trapped citizens. It consumed temples as well as tenements, and even the emperor's palace was not spared. Of the fourteen wards of the city only four remained untouched; the others were either totally destroyed or badly damaged.

Nero, the emperor, immediately began rebuilding the devastated city with lavish magnificence along the lines of a new master plan. But the more vigorously he devoted himself to urban reconstruction, the more his action seemed to substantiate the rumors that he himself had started the fire as the cheapest way to clear the site of his new city. Obviously such rumors did not endear the emperor to the thousands who had lost everything in the holocaust. To shift the blame from his own shoulders, he picked out a group of "foreigners" who were unable to offer resistance: the Christians.

According to Tacitus, the historian who reported all this, he could hardly have made a better choice. These Christians were "hated for their abominations." They were guilty, if not of setting the fire, at least of "hatred against mankind." They fully merited such "extreme and exemplary punishment." Whether merited or not, the penalty was meted out by both emperor and enraged populace. Those convicted of holding this faith were nailed to crosses. Or they were clothed in the skins of leopards or tigers and then thrown into the arena to be mauled by hunting dogs. Or they were dipped in pitch and set on fire to provide human torches, illuminating the emperor's gardens for public enjoyment. Such things happened to Christians in the very city where, within a decade, the Gospel of Mark was to be written for those who had survived the holocaust.

Where was Mark himself during these days? We do not know. But we do know that he had been colleague of Peter and Paul, both of whom, according to Clement, had probably been among the first to fall prey to Nero's sadism. How did their colleague, John Mark, manage to escape? We do not know. Perhaps he had been sent to Asia with letters and instructions for churches there (Col. 4:10). If so, he returned to Rome soon after their deaths. In any case we can be quite sure that he knew the story well and that he was courageous enough to continue his ministry among the survivors in the same city. In studying his record we need to keep this background in mind. We know all too little of the man himself, but we know that he was a minister of churches which had been riddled by persecution and tormented by inward divisions. He was writing for congregations which had lost their experienced leaders, and which were more than ever temped to a policy of care-fullness, in order to pacify the synagogue, the Roman populace, and the police force.

This turbulent situation was aggravated by another ominous development which began shortly after the death of the Apostles. In Judea the Jewish community became embroiled in a bitter and bloody effort to oust the Roman troops and to expel the provincial rulers. Their revolt developed into a full-scale war against the Goliath of the West. For four years the futile battle lasted, until Jerusalem itself was captured and destroyed by the Roman army in A.D. 70. What effects did this war have on churches which had so recently been branded as traitors? Roman minds, of course, linked the Christians more closely to the Jews than to any other group.

The course of the war must therefore have fanned the flames of suspicion. Even within the churches, loyalties must have been severely tested and the lines between Jew and Gentile painfully sharp. How strongly should Jewish Christians support their kinsmen in Jerusalem who were starving and dying during the siege by Roman mercenaries? How vigorously should they cultivate their neighbors in Rome? With whom should the Christians ally themselves when they had so recently suffered from both Romans and Jews?

It was at about the time of this Jewish war, in the midst of such conditions, that the Gospel of Mark was written by a man who had been in close touch with all that had happened: John Mark. Let us summarize what had happened to him. A native of Jerusalem, Mark had at a very early date joined the ranks of followers of Jesus. He had been associated, as we have noted, with the apostolic work of both Peter and Paul. He had visited many churches in all parts of the empire. He had lived through imprisonments; he had seen friends and leaders martyred; he had for several years been at work among Roman Christians who had experienced for at least thirty years the difficulties of following a crucified Lord. Such an author writing to such churches produced this Gospel.

Mark was probably a Jew, well versed in the Law and the Prophets, acquainted with the traditions and customs of the Judean homeland and bound by many strong ties to the hope of Israel. He was a Jewish Christian, whose life had been turned upside down by the story of Jesus the Messiah. He had interpreted discipleship as an inescapable call to be a witness and had devoted many years to preaching the gospel in Asia, Achaia, and other Roman provinces. His work had been similar to that of Peter and Paul, and, like theirs, it had carried him into intimate fellowship with Gentile congregations and therefore into the cross fire of opposition from synagogues and even from other Jewish Christians. He had done his best to heal the schism between Christians of left and right wing—a task which was as difficult in Rome as anywhere else.

In our study of the Gospel, we must be as concerned with the first readers of this book as with its author. What were they like? Why would they find the book of interest and value? How would they react to the story told by their own brother and leader? One thing is clear: before reading this Gospel they had already accepted the gospel. They had accepted as Lord a Jew of Nazareth who had been condemned and executed as a criminal by the Roman governor, Pontius Pilate. They knew how this Jew had attracted at once the enmity of Jewish leaders in Palestine and the passionate loyalty of Jewish laymen—fishermen, farmers, tradesmen. All of them in Rome who had accepted baptism in the name of Jesus had jeopardized their standing with both the Jewish and pagan communities there. They would have accepted some degree of fellowship with those Christian leaders in Rome, whether Jew or Gentile, who had so alienated the populace and police. Mark was writing, then, to baptized believers who were living near the center of a maelstrom of human passions, near the frontiers where men daily faced death. The Gospel was written by and for pilgrims of faith in a crucified Messiah. Imagining what it was like to live as such pilgrims may prepare us for studying this book, because rightly considered it is a part of the dialogue which transpired between the man John Mark and the believers who lived in Rome. The more fully we enter into that dialogue the more fully we will understand Mark's story.

Mark's Intentions

We cannot unlock the meaning of any written document unless we understand the motives of its author. The motives are the keys. Why should he have written anything at all? What difference would his book make in the situation of his first readers? At what points did he want them to share his knowledge and his convictions? Sometimes all we need to say about a book is simply this: "The book is itself a plain answer to these questions. This is what the author wanted to say and he said it." Although this is true of Mark, there are other things which we can say about his motives.

We can say, for instance, that he felt impelled to write this book because of his own loyalty to Jesus. Like other Christian leaders, he thought of himself as a slave of Jesus Christ, compelled by love to tell the story of his Master. He had himself been instructed by those memories of Jesus which had been relayed to him by other disciples. From various episodes in Jesus' ministry Mark had received courage and joy, a sense of direction for living, insights on how to meet the varying trials of faith. He wanted to share such insights.

We must go on to say that, like other servants of Christ, Mark had been assigned to minister to the needs of the churches. Once we have imagined ourselves living in the Rome of his day, we will recognize how varied were those needs, and how difficult to meet. Each disciple confronted numerous personal dilemmas as he tried to embody his loyalty to Christ in the daily situation. Each congregation was caught up in a welter of problems in which efforts to establish church discipline often tended to split the congregation. We have seen how steps taken to advance the mission of the Church often heightened the hostility of Jewish and Roman officials. Effort to increase mutual hospitality among the scattered congregations encountered the inertia of long-standing isolations and prejudices. Yet that effort had to be made.

Then, as always, one need was to keep all minds focused on the call to discipleship which Christ had issued. This call had come to each disciple when for the first time he had heard the story of Jesus as the Son of God. The story had reached its climax in the death of Jesus as a ransom for many. In the forsakenness on the cross, in the darkness that shrouded the whole earth, his power as the Son of God had been most luminously disclosed. The narrative of this event, therefore, occupied the largest single section of the Gospel (Mark 14:1 to the end). All that came before it is prelude: an extension of the story backwards, sufficiently full to make the significance of the Cross clear. What came after it was postlude: the witness of the Apostles to the Risen Lord and the story of the Church; these Mark did not attempt to relate, at least in this particular document.

Many various impulses may have induced Mark to commit to writing the Passion Story, with this necessary prelude. The chief Apostles, in whose sermons this story had from the first been the heart, had now suffered a martyr's death like their Master's. To put into writing their witness to the Cross would both safeguard that witness from undue change and fittingly commemorate their own faithfulness. To tell again, for reiterated use in the churches, the gist of their apostolic testimony would provide a continuing pattern for those who inherited their mission to the world. This story would serve as the spearhead of evangelism, calling all men to repentance and faith. By repentance, those who heard the story would identify themselves with those who had crucified Jesus and for whom he had died. By faith in him as God's Son they would accept his self-offering as nothing less than God's power made available for the world's redemption.

Mark could not, in fact, say anything about Jesus without

throwing some light upon the conditions of discipleship in Rome a full generation after Jesus' death. This is why the first disciples of Jesus played so important a role in Mark's narrative. Their involvement in the events was more than incidental or accidental; it was essential. Because Mark was interested in Jesus, he could not avoid being interested in the men whom he enlisted. Therefore Mark shows how Jesus' work as Messiah had begun with the call of four men to fish for other men (1:16-20). Jesus could not, in Mark's view, announce God's Kingdom without issuing this summons. And very soon thereafter, from the whole band of followers Jesus selected twelve "to be with him, and to be sent out to preach" (3:14). If Jesus could not preach the good news without calling for followers, those who believed him could not long follow him without receiving the mandate to preach. Their work as newscasters, in turn, could not be accomplished without issuing the same summons for others to repent and to believe. The story of the beginning of the gospel was thus shown to be inseparable from the story of the beginning of discipleship and of the formation of the Church as Jesus' family (3:35). It is significant that the disciples were absent from none of the episodes recounted by Mark except the baptism of Jesus in the Jordan and the fulfillment of this baptism on Golgotha. Yet even in those events their lives were entangled in a deeper sense, for Jesus was being baptized for them. Mark could therefore not tell the story of Jesus without telling the story of Jesus' first disciples.

But there were practical reasons for doing this, in addition to the historical reasons. Each story in which Peter and John had been actors became a story in which the disciples in the Roman churches were present through their identification with Peter and John. The battles between Jesus and Satan remained current history because the believers in Rome were caught in the same vortex of conflict; their loyalty to the living Jesus exposed them to onslaughts from the same Adversary. When Jesus had corrected the blindness and stubbornness of the Twelve, he had included their successors, too. So in Mark's account of how the Twelve had learned to follow Jesus to the cross, every later disciple could find disturbing examples and austere instruction. Mark had intended it that way. To his whole Gospel he applied what Jesus had made explicit at a climactic moment: "What I say to you I say to all" (13:37). As laymen, the Twelve had heard what Jesus, and Mark, had wanted all later laymen to hear.

These Twelve, however, were not only laymen but also Apostles. As the first leaders they provided the clearest pattern for leaders in later generations. Because Jesus had trained the Twelve as his accredited representatives, every later missionary and evangelist could learn from their story the ABC's of his own task. For example, when Mark told how the Twelve had competed with one another for top honors (10:35-37), he could not avoid thinking of all sorts of quarrels among later leaders. With his experience of working with the Apostles, Mark had access to information about what had happened before Golgotha; he also had access to the experience of the Twelve on the mission field and to the subsequent experiences of Apostles in Rome. He therefore told the stories about Jesus with one eye on the dilemmas and opportunities faced by leaders of his own day.

These dilemmas, as we have seen, often took the form of intra-church conflicts which were prompted by the wish to keep peace with the police. Roman Christians could not for a moment forget the suspicions of the Roman government. In telling the stories of Jesus, Mark reminded them of how Jesus and the Twelve had incurred the hostility of the same government. For this reason, Mark took a special interest in what had been said and done by the centurion in Galilee, by the Roman puppet Herod, and by Pilate, the procurator in Judea. He did not fail to tell of the trial, the verdict, the mocking and scourging, the cruel execution. Nor could a Roman Christian read that story without recalling the edicts of Claudius and Nero and preparing himself for a repetition of the same fate. In telling the good news, Mark could not forget how frightened the disciples had been in the storm-tossed boat, how much they had dreaded that last trip to Jerusalem, how frantically they had betrayed their Master by leaping into the darkness when he was arrested. Nor could his readers ignore the relevance of such anecdotes to their own daily fears. Mark was quite aware of this relevance. In fact, he desired to tell each episode so simply and so clearly that each reader would read himself right into its center and recognize himself in its actors.

We have already noticed that trouble with the pagan government was almost always linked to trouble with the Jewish synagogues. Christians who wanted to avoid trouble with one usually wanted to avoid trouble with the other. The Christian community was caught between two obligations. On the one hand, because Jesus was the Messiah of Israel, who had come to fulfill God's promises to Israel, they were obliged to carry his message to all the sons of Israel. They could not repudiate their Jewish foes; they must rather try to win them to their rightful King. On the other hand, the Messiah had upset the Law and rejected the traditions, had been repudiated by the scribes and condemned by the Sanhedrin. His disciples were therefore obliged to join in this revolutionary path, even though it meant hatred from their own synagogues and kinsmen. What was the best course to follow? Mark believed that the answer could be discerned in the debates between Jesus and the Pharisees. To him, the story of the Cross was unintelligible apart from the stories of all the controversies with the Jewish leaders which made the Cross inevitable. By what authority had Jesus done these things? By the power of Beelzebul? Why had he eaten with unwashed hands? Why had he defiled the Sabbath? Why had he consorted with sinners and tax collectors? Why had he claimed authority over the Temple? Why had he set aside the commandments of the Law? Why had he encouraged his disciples to do likewise?

By telling the stories of Jesus' debates with his antagonists, Mark was also telling the story of the Church's debates with the synagogue and the story of debates within the churches concerning the relationships between the gospel and the Law. Mark intended to do this, in part through loyalty to Jesus himself and in part through loyalty to his brothers in Christ who were placed in situations where daily temptations and decisions ran strangely parallel to those of the earlier day.

In summary, we may say that Mark had many purposes in collecting the anecdotes about Jesus and in editing them into a single story. Noting the personnel in each episode may alert us to a recognition of these purposes. Every reference to Jesus threw light upon the requirements incumbent upon every disciple, upon the conflicts within every congregation, and upon each congregation's difficult mission to the world. Every reference to the disciples held its significance either for apostolic leaders or for ordinary believers, or for both. Every reference to the crowd, as being astonished or offended, suggested both the initial audiences for the gospel message and contemporary audiences. Mark wrote his Gospel so that the wealth of the gospel's meaning and the depth of its power might be made more accessible to the Christians in Rome.

Mark's Message

Mark had a message which he wished to share with the members of the Roman churches. If this had not been true, he would not have produced a document at all. Books of this size and importance do not appear without specific reasons. What this message was, however, is not so easily determined. In a sense, this whole document was the message he wished to convey. He wanted churches to have available for frequent use this whole cycle of stories and teachings.

It is very difficult, accordingly, to reduce his message to any statement shorter than his own. He did not ask himself first what message he wanted to give and then how he could give it most effectively. He did not first make a point and then search for anecdotes to illustrate and to support it. He did not state a case and then prove it. But why not?

When we try to answer that question, we begin to realize that this is indeed a very strange kind of document, different from every earlier type of story and in fact quite different even from the other books in the New Testament which later came to be called Gospels. Yet there are certain traits which these four books have in common, and these traits tell us why we cannot separate the message from the narrative as a whole.

For example, the Gospel writer is concerned simply to recount what God has done, not for the storyteller alone or through him, but for the world through his chosen Son, Jesus of Nazareth. The writer is therefore himself more the recipient than the narrator of the story, more its servant than its master.

Moreover, the deeds done by Jesus and the recital of those deeds have come to the writer through various channels. The Apostles, themselves "eyewitnesses and ministers of the word" (Luke 1:1-4), had recited the deeds of Jesus on numerous occasions. Men like Mark and Luke had heard their predecessors recount memories of what Jesus had said and done, of what men had said and done to him. These memories became traditions, and these traditions were common property, not the special creation of a particular writer.

When Mark combined these memories and traditions into a single consecutive story (and he was probably the first person to do so), he used materials with which his audience was familiar. They had heard the gospel before they read the Gospel. They had heard accounts of Jesus' baptism, his ministry, his climactic visit to Jerusalem, his death, his meetings with his disciples after his resurrection. They already had heard "the preaching of Christ" and had responded with "the word of faith" (Rom. 10:17, 8). This word had proved to be as near to them as their own heart and lips. In short, before composing his story with his pen, Mark had shared with his audience the memory of the "beginning of the gospel" (Mark 1:1). He was bound to his audience by the same faith, the same baptism, the same vocation, the same Lord, the same Spirit. By gathering their mutual memories into a single, consecutive recital, he would remind himself and them of the basic Covenant into which they had entered. They had heard the word before, but they needed to listen to it again. They needed to catch anew the implications of Jesus' baptism for their own faith and work. They needed to see more clearly the links between what had happened in the story of Jesus and what was happening in their own story as Roman disciples. So Mark sought to meet these needs by retelling the stories in such a way as to accent their relevance to the varied opportunities and obstacles faced by servants of Christ in Nero's Rome.

We can perhaps come closest to Mark's conception of this relevance by choosing the word "gospel" and by describing what meanings this term conveyed when seen from three different angles: as the news which Jesus had announced, as the news which his Apostles had announced, and as the inauguration of a New Covenant between God and men through the ministry of Jesus and his Apostles.

The News of God Which Jesus Had Announced

In his story Mark takes his readers back in time to those days, and back in space to those places, in which Jesus had first announced a message about God's action. Readers therefore need to follow the story from this angle. When Jesus had come into Galilee, he had begun his work by shouting "the gospel" or "the good news" of God (Mark 1:14). Then, as now, news meant that something had happened, something which made a difference, something which changed decisively the situation in which men were standing. News of God meant that this something had been done by God. By his action God had altered the situation, altered it in such a way as to alter all situations. The newscaster must therefore tell what God had done and was still doing. But he could not do this unless he had seen and heard what God had done, and unless God had authorized him to tell others what he had seen and heard. The newscaster must first be appointed by God as his prophet and empowered by God to speak to men as his interpreter. Only with such authorization and power could the words and deeds of the prophet point beyond themselves to the immediate intentions of the Most High. Before Jesus had begun his work he had received this authority and power. He had seen and heard what God was doing—a prophetic vision. He had been called and sent by God with power to speak and to act in accordance with God's purposes—a prophetic vocation. In his opening verses, Mark tells with extreme terseness the story of this vision and this vocation.

What had Jesus seen and heard before he announced with authority, "The time is fulfilled"? (1:15). What had enabled him to know that the period of preparation had been completed, that God had come to the point of fulfilling the promise which he had earlier given to his people? We may not know the complete answers to such questions, but we can see what Mark believed was essential to that answer. God's pledge, given to Israel in the prophets, had at last been redeemed. He had sent Elijah again to his people (John the Baptizer) with an authority direct from heaven (9:13; 11:30). In the baptism of repentance which this Elijah had preached, in the forgiveness of sins which accompanied the contrition and baptism of Israel, God had given an authentic sign that the time of waiting was over (1:4-8). The work of John the Baptizer, embodied in the contrition, baptism, and forgiveness of God's Israel, had marked the end of the epoch which God had ordained as preparation.

This epoch had now given way to a new epoch in which God had sent his Spirit, baptizing his people with the powers of the coming Kingdom. Jesus had seen and heard the descent of this very Spirit, a sign to him that had enabled him to proclaim with confidence: "The kingdom of God is at hand" (1:15). This sign had been disclosed when he had accepted the baptism proclaimed by John with divine authority. Then Jesus had seen the heavens opened. He had been granted a vision of those heights and depths of reality where God's invisible deeds were already shaping the later course of earthly events. From the opened heavens he had seen God's Spirit descending—sign of the accomplishment on earth of what God had already initiated in heaven. God's Kingdom at that very moment had invaded earth's territory. The Spirit had descended on Jesus himself, a clear token of his own appointment as one through whom the powers of the Kingdom had begun to operate. Henceforth he must speak and act out of this mysterious authority from heaven (11:30) communicated by the Spirit and indicative of God's intention to share his favor and his grace with men. The Kingdom was at hand because God's Spirit had appeared with power among men. (For a similar picture of the heaven's opening, and of the Spirit conferring authority on the prophet, see Revelation 1:10-11; 4:1-2.)

This power, however, had been effective not in the termination of struggle, but in its initiation. The Spirit had not invited Jesus into an ideal Utopia but had driven him into the wilderness, to engage there in a strange warfare. The Kingdom's approach had precipitated a fearful battle between God and Satan. The battlefield could be described as both the wilderness of superhuman conflict and the very human heart of Jesus of Nazareth. What Jesus had seen and heard at the Jordan was given a terrifying authentication in what happened in this wilderness. His baptism plunged him into lonely combat with the wily Prince of Evil—Satan himself. If, in this combat, the ruler of all the demonic forces had won, that victory would have made nonsense of the news of God's Kingdom (3:27-29). But Satan had been overcome. And that defeat had proved to Jesus the reality of the Spirit's power, and the new accessibility of God's Kingdom. Henceforth, he took any denial of the Spirit's presence to be an act of blasphemy against God. God had actually begun to plunder Satan's dominion. He had demonstrated his power to free men's hearts from demonic controls. He had sent his Spirit to extend the range of forgiveness and freedom. And Jesus was the messenger, fully authorized to proclaim the news because he had fully met and vanquished the Devil. This was what had happened. This was what enabled Jesus to proclaim that the time of preparation had been completed and that the new order had been inaugurated. The King of the world had established by his edict a new government. Henceforth all human affairs must be conducted on the basis of this new system, now declared to be in effect. This edict was good news for all who wished a victory over the demonic powers on God's terms, bad news for Satan and for all who wanted release on other terms than God's.

What were the terms which the King had specified? "Repent, and believe in the gospel" (1:15). This twin command corroborated the announcement which the prophet John had relayed from heaven: repentance for the forgiveness of sins (1:4). Jesus continued to relay this same demand, no longer merely as preparation for a coming judgment, but now as a necessary response to the fact that God had made his forgiveness available to sinners. Therefore, the twin command received a quite new accent: men must trust joyfully in what God had now done. God had already introduced his power among men by defeating Satan and by releasing men from their captivity to him. To trust in this good news brought men within the range where the Spirit was in control. It also gave them an essential share in the temptation of Jesus. By believing in the good news, men opened themselves to bitter attacks by Satan, but they discovered therein how the Spirit could overcome the powers of darkness.

These were God's terms for those who would receive his Kingdom: repentance and joyful trust in the good news which Jesus proclaimed. The opening verses of Mark introduce the basic thrust of these terms. The rest of the document spells out the meaning of the terms to those whom Jesus has called as followers. The twin command is Mark's summary of all the commands. The basic terms remained the same, although the words changed and the shape of obedience changed in accordance with the shape of the Devil's resistance.

Those who repented accepted their place in Jesus' baptism and in his humiliation. This required the surrender of personal ambitions and the adoption of God's standard of greatness (10:35-45). It meant instant readiness to detect and to resist the temptations of Satan, who subtly suggested at every step that the disciple seek easier forms of obedience (4:15; 8:33). It meant the endurance of bitter tribulation and brutal persecution because of the Word (4:17). It meant a thorough rejection of anxiety over earthly fortunes. The Word, by its very nature, excluded delight in riches and desires for prestige and security (4:19; 10:27-28). Repentance took on the shape of Jesus' own obedience, the shape of total self-denial and self-renunciation, the shape of investing all hopes in the dawn of the new day (3:35; 8:34-38; 10:29-30).

Satan had one great advantage: How could any news be considered good when it cost so much? How could God demand that men pay this price? Considering what this news demanded, its acceptance was nothing short of miraculous. Jesus knew well (as did Mark) that to trust wholly in this news was quite impossible for men (10:27). But it was possible for God to enable men to hear Jesus' voice as being indeed the voice of God himself (1:22-27; 2:10). Those who heard were empowered to share Jesus' own joy over the miracle of God's forgiveness of sins, God's power over Satan, God's desire to cleanse the lepers and the insane. Faith in such goodness on the part of God gave his hearers power to forgive their own enemies—all of them and the worst of them (11:20-26). Was it hard for the disciples to do this? Of course it was, tremendously hard. But faith in God's news produced confidence that God's Word would continue to reap its appointed harvest. Though God's elect be slain (as John had been, 9:13), their endurance to the end would mean their salvation (13:13). Jesus himself would be slain, but his message concerning God's salvation would survive even the passing away of heaven and earth (13:31). Could men believe such news? Not without accepting Jesus' promise as being so true that it displaced the authority of the leaders ordained to govern Israel (12:9), the sanctity of God's Temple and its worship (11:17; 13:2), and the demands of the holy Law (2:27; 7:1-13). Belief in the good news of God catapulted believers into the very center of this revolution in human affairs.

What evidence did Jesus give to prove that this revolution had begun? The evidence was far from obvious. Jesus gave his own word as evidence, but who could accept a word which cost so much and which was challenged by so many? Jesus gave his own deeds as evidence, but who could see these deeds as more impressive than the march of Roman armies and the power of empires? Yet even when Jesus moved along his inconspicuous way, a few individuals seemed eager to believe him. Who were they? A nameless woman who anointed Jesus' head for his burial (14:3-9), a poor widow who cast into the Temple treasury every cent she had (12:41-44), men and women driven to despair by demons (1:32-34, 39), lepers who had no home among men (1:40-45), prostitutes and traitorous tax collectors whom the good people had ostracized, the "dead" who had nothing left but God's grace, and here or there a disciple who had begun to move from one act of obedience toward the next. Mark does nothing to minimize the strangeness of the story.

Mark did not play down the strangeness of the revolution which Jesus had announced; in fact, he stressed it. How? By making clear at each turn of the page how people of every class and

condition had rejected the news. To be sure, men had now and
again been amazed by the authority with which Jesus had cast out
demons (1:21-27), yet this amazement had usually turned into
rejection rather than faith. Jesus' assurance that God had forgiven
sinners was interpreted as blasphemy (2:7). His friendship for
outcasts, his repudiation of the Law, his liberation of the demon-
possessed—all in the name of Israel's God—had alienated the
leaders of Israel. Their loyalty to the Law had impelled them to
plot his death (2:16; 3:2, 6; 3:22). Those in his own town, his rela-
tives and neighbors, had been unable to fathom the mystery (6:1-
6). The longer he pursued his task, the longer grew the roster of
enemies: Herod and his supporters, the synagogue leaders, the
Temple and its governors, Pilate and his soldiers, even his own
disciples. At the end he was rejected by all, helpless and forsaken.
The terms of God's revolution had indeed proved too rigorous.
Faith in it had become altogether impossible for men (10:27).
Jesus had been unable to show his own generation any sign convincing enough to induce among them the kind of repentance and
faith which God demanded. But he had accomplished one thing:
he had made his death a test of the truth of what he had said and
done. Henceforth, the proclamation of his death by those whom
God should summon would be the means by which the fact of
revolution would be attested. His own announcement of the good
news of what God had done would be continued in their announcement. Heaven and earth would pass away, but not his
word.

We suggest now to the reader that this would be a good point at
which to take Mark's Gospel, to read it through slowly, and to ask
himself how well the successive episodes do, in fact, embody the
news which Jesus had announced.

The Good News of Jesus Christ Which the Apostles Announced

We have examined the full meaning of the slogan which Jesus
had placed over his work: the good news of God. After his death
the Apostles placed over their ministry a similar slogan: "The gospel [good news] of Jesus Christ, the Son of God" (1:1). This second slogan, adopted by Mark, stands as the very title of his book.
We now wish to make clear what he had in mind in selecting it.

The message which Jesus proclaimed before Golgotha can at
certain points be distinguished from the gospel which the Apostles
proclaimed after that event. He had been called and authorized by

God; they had been called and authorized by the Risen Lord. Jesus' loyalty had centered on obedience to the heavenly King; their loyalty had been made possible by the King's Son. His news had dealt with God's work, theirs with the work of the exalted Christ. His ministry had ended in a crucifixion which had seemed to discredit his message about God; their ministry had begun, they had been in fact ordained to it, when God had shown them how much power he had given to the Crucified. Earlier, men had rejected the news by discounting Jesus' authority; now they would reject the news by discounting the Apostles' authority. The good news had become the word which they preached about Jesus Christ. It is the beginning of that word which we have before us in Mark's Gospel. For the full title of Mark's document as it left his hand was "The beginning of the gospel of Jesus Christ, the Son of God" (1:1). This is the new book of Genesis, the origins of that message about Christ which his Apostles preached in Jerusalem, Corinth, and Rome.

Notice, now, how the beginning of the task of the Apostles ran parallel to that of Jesus Christ. The task of the Messiah had begun in a threefold event: an authentic vision of heaven expressed in a word of God spoken from heaven with absolutely inescapable authority; the descent of the Spirit from heaven, carrying power to accomplish on earth what God had prepared in heaven; the experience of lonely struggle with Satan in the wilderness, a struggle in which the Spirit gave a decisive victory. This was the beginning. It was this three-sided event which authorized Jesus to teach, to preach, to heal, and to enlist men for God's mission to the world. Of his work this was the beginning.

Where may we locate a similar beginning for the work of the Apostles? How were they to receive a comparable authority and power? Without that authority they could not proclaim the Kingdom. And that authority required participation in the same kind of event. They needed a vision of heaven opened to disclose God's purposes. They needed a voice from heaven assigning them their task. They needed the power of the Spirit, descending from heaven, to enable them to vanquish the Devil, a victory which would yield its harvest in power to forgive sins, to fish for men, to face their own Golgothas with joy.

Does Mark tell us this story? No, not the whole story. He limits himself to its beginning. He does not give us, at least not in the present edition with its abrupt close at 16:8, any account of the

Apostles' vision, of their appointment to the task, of their victory over Satan, of their calling men into the New Age as heirs of the New Kingdom. We do not know the reasons for this omission. It is possible that he did actually include it and that the postscript to his story has been accidentally lost. Possibly he did not tell it because the Apostles themselves were in the habit, at this point in their preaching, of giving their own account of their appointment, using the confessional first person ("we," I Cor. 15:8-11). Possibly he did not want to tell it because his conception of his task was to carry the story only through the Passion of Jesus, leaving the Passion of the Apostles for other narrators. But in any case, Mark had the later story of the apostolic preaching in mind all the while he was telling about the Messiah's preaching. At frequent intervals he pointed ahead to that later story. He enabled readers to see how the Apostles' preaching about Jesus Christ was based upon this beginning, those events which reached from the Jordan to the empty tomb.

Let us be more specific. When Jesus had begun his work he had called the Apostles from their nets to follow him and to learn how to fish for men. They had followed, although the new fishing may have been delayed until after their apprenticeship was complete. The basis of their following him had been at first Jesus' message about God's Kingdom, not about himself as God's Son. Like his, their initial work had been to proclaim the Kingdom and to call sinners to repentance (1:38; 2:17; 3:13-19; 6:7-13). To Mark these events had proved extremely significant: the call to follow, the period spent with Jesus, the commission to preach the Kingdom and to cast out demons. But this significance had not become clear until after Jesus was taken away from them. To be sure, he had tried to communicate to them the secrets of the Kingdom of God but had found their minds too obdurate (ch. 4). He had encouraged them to use their own resources for feeding the hungry sheep, but, alas, they were quite without the power to serve as shepherds (chs. 6, 8). Obeying his command they had gone to various towns, preaching the Kingdom. It had not, however, occurred to them to proclaim *Jesus*. The demons had recognized in him a heavenly authority greater than Satan. Not so the disciples. "They did not understand ... their hearts were hardened" (6:52).

An important shift had come in the episodes recounted in the eighth and ninth chapters. "On the way" (that road of the Messiah which Mark saw as leading only to Calvary), Jesus had invited a discussion concerning himself (8:27). The impetuous disclosure by Peter that Jesus was indeed the Messiah had been accompanied by four strange and even shocking echoes: First, Jesus had commanded them to keep silent about him (8:30). Second, he immediately had told them of his coming rejection, death, and resurrection. Third, Peter's protest against such a fate for Jesus had prompted the strongest of rebukes. Fourth, Jesus had announced that every disciple must carry a cross. All this Jesus had insisted upon, but its truth was lost upon them. It could become God's truth for them only after their Master had died. The beginning of their work had been anchored in the early days with Jesus, but this beginning could first become a genuine beginning for preaching the gospel only after Jesus' suffering had been accomplished.

To be sure, Mark included in the earlier stories intimations of this later climactic authorization. In the account of the Transfiguration (9:2-13), for example, three disciples had experienced a vision of heavenly reality. While on a mountain they had seen Jesus clothed in heavenly attire, speaking with Moses and Elijah. They had heard God's own voice, the same voice which had spoken in Jesus' baptism, commanding them to obey Jesus. Yet this was not the moment when they had received power for their ministry. The Spirit had not yet come upon them, a deficiency made painfully obvious by the very next encounter with demons. Jesus had ordered them not to speak of what they had seen until after the Resurrection. Only the Resurrection could make intelligible and release the power which had indeed been latent in their days with Jesus. The disclosure of Jesus talking with Moses and Elijah, the voice of God commanding obedience to his Son, these things would make sense only after the Son had died and had been raised from the dead. God's power which had operated in Jesus must first be released through the Risen Lord before the disciples would be fully empowered to proclaim the good news about Jesus Christ. Until then he must teach them about his suffering; until then they would fail to understand (9:30-32).

Over and over again, Mark carefully noted the forecasts which Jesus had made concerning what would soon happen to the disciples. At Jesus' arrest they would frantically run away—yet later they would stand before governors and kings "for my sake, to bear testimony before them" (13:9). Accused by a menial in Pilate's household of being friends of Jesus, they would swear, "I never knew him"—yet later they would be instrumental in preaching the gospel to all nations (13:10). While their Master was in direst agony they were unable to stay awake—yet later they would watch through the long nights for the Master to return (13:35). They would scatter like sheep at the Shepherd's death—yet the Shepherd would go before them to Galilee (14:27-28). There they would see him (16:7); and seeing him, they would drink the cup again with him (14:25). They would see ample signs of the coming of God's Kingdom with power. They would become in fact the fishers of men (1:17) whom Jesus had called, and they would call men by proclaiming the good news about Jesus Christ the Son of God. All this is included in Mark's title: "The beginning . . ." (1:1).

Here again a rereading of the entire Gospel of Mark at a single sitting is desirable, with each reader thinking of the entire document as the place where such Apostles as Peter and Paul would begin their addresses in the Roman Forum.

The Covenant with God

There is a third aspect of Mark's message which is as significant as the first two. We should read his document as his way of describing the New Covenant which God has inaugurated with men through the ministry of Jesus and his Apostles.

Mark's first readers had never heard Jesus preach. Perhaps none of them was an Apostle. Many of his readers must have heard an Apostle preach, but that number was rapidly decreasing as the years succeeded Nero's purge. To the degree, then, that this document focused on the preaching of the Apostles, it might exert a diminishing attraction after all the Apostles had died. Mark must keep in mind the whole company of Christians and write in such a way as to include them.

One way of doing this, as we have noted, was to write about the Twelve in such fashion that every disciple in Rome could see himself in their shoes. When Mark told of the specifications Jesus had set for companions, he made those specifications binding on all: total repentance, eager watchfulness, fearless trust, ruthless self-denial. So, too, when Mark described the anxieties and stupidities, the cautiousness and the greed of the Twelve, he knew that no disciple was immune and that no disciple would feel superior to the Twelve.

But Mark had another way of including all later disciples within the covers of his book. He tells the story of the inauguration of an eternal Covenant between Jesus and disciples of every generation. This story covered sixteen chapters, yet it also could be condensed into a dozen words: "This is my blood of the covenant, which is poured out for many" (14:24). Roman Christians in Mark's day were accustomed to drink this cup, to participate in this supper. This Covenant had been sealed with them just as fully as with the Twelve in the Upper Room. Christ had been as fully present with them; he had just as certainly given them the cup. Mark believed this. Therefore there is special significance in how he tells the story. When he makes a special point of Judas' presence at the table, he is thinking of the table in every city and year. Judas is there. Mark makes it clear that Jesus poured out this Covenant for men who were about to flee in cowardly hysteria. We can almost hear him add, "If this was the case with Peter and John, how much more the case with you?" With his eyes both on the Twelve and on his Roman friends, Mark tells of disciples whose typical responses are those of fear and guilt, shiftiness and unpreparedness. But he also tells of a Christ who proclaims God's forgiveness of sins, and who demonstrates that forgiveness by pouring out for them the blood of the Covenant.

Mark gives careful attention to another form of this Covenant —that expressed by baptism. The Roman Christians had been baptized with Jesus' baptism. What did this mean to Mark? It meant that Jesus had established a binding Covenant with them, the significance of which appears in Mark's account of a dialogue on the road to the Cross (10:32-45). The baptism which Jesus had begun in the Jordan was to be completed in the Crucifixion. Disciples are expected by Jesus to accept the same baptism. It is characteristic of the Twelve, however, that they exaggerate their readiness for such a fate. But it is even more characteristic of Jesus to promise them, in spite of the self-deceptions, that they will ultimately join him in his baptism and drink his cup. They will learn from his death the only law of greatness (10:43-45); they will be bound to become slaves of all for his sake.

This Covenant we must view as the key to Mark's understanding of the nature of the Church and of its ministry to the world. The Church had not been far from Mark's mind when he pictured the first preaching of Jesus. It had been there in the Master's call and in the disciples' response of following. To Mark it had been significant that the call had come in the midst of daily and ordi-

nary routines and that it had challenged the hold which those routines exercised on men's minds (1:16-20). To Mark, however, it
was clear that Jesus had not limited his healing work to those who
followed "on the way." His power had been designed to help "all
who were sick or possessed with demons" (1:32). The impact of
the good news of God had extended into whatever regions Satan
had controlled. To be sure, Jesus had called disciples, he had
formed a new people, but he had done this in order to reach the
sick, the outcasts, the lepers, the harlots, and the traitors. It is
striking that Mark made no effort to restrict the healing work of
Jesus to the band of disciples. In fact, he tells not a single story of
Jesus healing a disciple. The area which God's redemptive power
had entered was much larger than the "Church." The Church was
simply the number of those who joined the Messiah in his ministry to the world.

It was this which made the disciples so different from other human groupings. For one thing, their attitudes toward sacred places
and sacred days had been changed. They now knew that the Temple could be found wherever Jesus ate with men. They knew that
he had become the Lord of the Sabbath (2:23-28). He had made
all foods clean (7:19). Mark saw the Church as a family composed of Jesus' brothers, sisters, and mother (3:31-35), made kin-
dred by devotion to the will of one Father. He saw it as the company of those who discovered in the storms of their journey the
presence of One who could command the wind and the sea (4:35-
41). This is the symbolic way in which Mark pictured the
Church. In all these pictures God's power creates the Church by
calling men and women into a new fellowship. In them all, Jesus
stands at the center, sharing with men his generosity and grace.

But Mark did not allow his readers to suppose that the work of
Jesus stopped at the circumference of this circle. On frequent occasions Jesus reminded his followers that his chief concern was
with the sheep who had no shepherd (6:34). The first business on
the disciples' agenda was to provide food for the multitudes
(6:30-44; 8:1-10). Those thousands were alone in the desert
without bread; when the disciples failed in their task Jesus would
feed them, but he did so after rebuking the disciples for their impotence. The "Church" itself was intended to be a company of
servants and not a select circle of people served by others
(10:45). In this regard as in others, the "Church" during Jesus'
ministry was unable to fulfill his expectations. In this regard as in

others, the Covenant could not become truly effective until Jesus himself had so drawn the circle as to include all sinners. This was the circle drawn by the Covenant in his blood. His followers could not honor this Covenant except by sharing his love for others.

This is the kind of community which God had created through the call of his Messiah. Mark saw the Church as constituted by that call. But he also knew that the Church could not exist apart from the ransom provided in Jesus' death. Just as the Apostles awaited the completion of Jesus' mission before they could begin to proclaim the good news, so, too, the family of Jesus awaited the drinking of his cup before the Covenant could be fully effective. The Passion Story was central, therefore, not only in the mission of Jesus and in the message of the Apostles but also in the everyday life of the Church. The centrality of the Passion was for Mark the basis for the regular observance of the Eucharist by the churches of Rome.

The power of the Last Supper did not lie in the merit of the Church, for all were guilty of denying the Lord. Rather it lay in the promise of Jesus to break bread with his brothers in the Kingdom of God, a promise that could be fulfilled only in his resurrection. But it would be fulfilled; in Mark's day it had been fulfilled. The builders had rejected the stone, but God had made it the cornerstone of his temple (12:10-11; 13:1-2). Mark saw the Church as this temple—"a house of prayer for all the nations" (11:17). Or, changing the figure, Mark thought of the Church as a tenant of God's vineyard, replacing the earlier tenants who had defaulted in their duty (12:9). The vineyard remained the same: God's people, where God produced and claimed the harvest. But the personnel of the caretakers had changed: the Church inherited the stewardship (12:1-9). It must preach the good news to all nations (13:10), accepting the hatred of all nations "for my name's sake," and enduring to the end (13:13). The Church was the company of God's elect, subject to all the temptations of Jesus himself, but recipients of the promise of a final harvesting (13:27) and of the command to watch for the Master's coming (13:37).

In Mark's eyes, then, the Covenant of the cup signified the sharing of the Church in the very mission on which Jesus had been sent: the Church received in Jesus' blood a vision of the Son of Man, a voice from heaven with its authorization to proclaim the good news, to heal the sick, to cast out demons, and to call all the nations to repentance and faith. This was the message which Mark

gave to the Roman churches—and in his mind it was the very
message which the Apostles had proclaimed from the beginning
of their baptism. Their message in turn had been the same as Jesus himself had proclaimed from the beginning of his baptism.
The Messiah, the Apostles, and the Church were thus bound together in a single Covenant community, bearing to the world the
fulfillment of God's promise.

The Structure of the Story

As a person reads this earliest of the Gospels, his eyes move
rapidly from paragraph to paragraph. The sequence of episodes
draws him onward toward the end. He is frequently unaware of
the literary form because of his obsession with the content. For
the reader, as certainly for the author, the message is everything;
by comparison the form attracts little notice. Nevertheless, the
structure of this document is not unimportant, and we should look
at it.

Mark did not create his materials out of his own mind; he inherited them. So completely did he depend upon common memories that it is almost impossible to detect his signature anywhere
in the document. Where this is true of a literary composition, the
best clue to the author's intentions will often be discovered in the
order and arrangement of the separate episodes and sayings.

So we ask about Mark's method of arranging the anecdotes
which he had received. Why did he combine the various episodes
in the order which we find? The first answer is obvious: he knew
how Jesus' ministry had begun, so he put those items first; he
knew how it had ended, so he put those memories last; he arranged the other episodes in between, even though in many cases
he had no fixed record concerning the proper location of many in-
tervening sayings and deeds.

We must therefore ask why Mark chose the sequence for these
materials which fell between the opening and the close of Jesus'
work. We may be aided at this point by the question: Where lies
the center of gravity in the book as a whole? As a person reads the
book rapidly, he discovers this magnetic center not in the earlier
chapters, nor in the middle span of stories, but at the end. The
reader's attention is magnetized toward the account of the very
last day, as found in chapters 14 and 15. (We should remember
that our chapter and verse divisions had not been introduced in

Mark's own writing.) From the Last Supper until the burial was a single day in his understanding, for the Jews measured days from sunset to sunset. In the record of this day, we notice a concentration of interest and suspense. Here the author gives more complete details than elsewhere. He also weaves the successive episodes very tightly together into a single dramatic whole. From the plot of the priests (14:1) to the entombment (15:46) the story moves forward with almost breathless haste in spite of its fullness of description. There is no doubt at all; this narrative provides the climax of the book.

We understand why this is so when we recall that Mark was a close companion of the Apostles and that the story of the death of Jesus constituted the invariable center of their preaching. The writer Luke furnishes us with records of that preaching in the Book of Acts. Entirely typical is the following as a sermon climax:

> "The God . . . of our fathers . . . glorified his servant Jesus, whom you delivered up and denied in the presence of Pilate, when he had decided to release him. But you denied the Holy and Righteous One, and asked for a murderer to be granted to you, and killed the Author of life . . ." (Acts 3:13-15a).

Or if we wish firsthand evidence from one of the Apostles, we should listen to this: "I decided to know nothing among you except Jesus Christ and him crucified" (I Cor. 2:2). Like Paul, Mark knew nothing but Jesus crucified. To him the account of the arrest, the denial, the Crucifixion, was the center of the gospel which the Apostles preached, and therefore the center of his story.

From this center we should think of Mark as working backward, and as arranging everything else in such a way as to lead most surely to this climax. He added first the accounts of Jesus' journey to the Holy City and of what had happened there (chs. 11-13). Christians wanted to know what events had led to the plot and to the arrest. In this section, alone in all his document, Mark takes pains to preserve a daily sequence from the entry into Jerusalem until the visit of the women to the tomb (11:1—16:8). This might be called the Larger Passion. In this section Mark brought together materials of varying kinds and diverse sources. He retold the memories of how Jesus had arrived in the city as its Messiah, how he had come to the Temple as its Lord, how he had sought to cleanse it and to restore its original purpose. These stories epitomized the paradox of faith that this Messiah had been responsible for both the destruction and the salvation of the Holy City and the Temple. Between the Messianic act of cleansing the Temple (11:15-19) and the Messianic act of promising the Temple's destruction (13:1-2), Mark inserted seven stories of a sort different both in form and origin. These are accounts of Jesus' debates with his adversaries, the Herodians and the Sadducees, and especially the scribes and Pharisees (11:27—12:44). These short anecdotes had probably served the Apostles as sermon illustrations for their countless debates with leaders of the synagogue. They gave Jesus' answers and those of the Church to challenges such as these: What was the source of his authority and theirs? How had he betrayed his people, and how had they? Who was he, and how might they test his credentials? Located in the larger context of the Passion these conflicts between the Messiah and his people answer the basic question of why the Son of Man had to die.

Located between these debates with Jesus' adversaries and the redemptive events of Supper and Cross, a collection of sayings appears, addressed to his disciples (13:3-37). This moment gave Jesus opportunity to prepare them for their own trials. He chose as the classroom the Mount of Olives, overlooking the city where he must die. In their minds, as well as in his, was the anticipation of stormy times ahead. At this strategic moment he answered questions which were to haunt them during their own careers: What will be the sign when all these things are to be accomplished? How will we recognize the coming of the Son of Man? What shall we do when we are beaten in synagogues and handed over to governors and kings? What are we to do when the world turns against us and we are left alone? It is to deal with such problems that Mark placed here this small collection of predictions and demands. To summarize all the commands he uses the simple order: "Watch."

We have now examined the method by which Mark organized the materials which were available to him into a consecutive narrative of Jesus' last week:

1. Symbolic narratives of the Messiah's entry into city and Temple (11:1-26).
2. A collection of controversies between Jesus and his adversaries (11:27—12:44).
3. A collection of sayings outlining the coming dangers and duties of disciples in their own Passion (13:3-37).

4. A tightly knit series of stories covering Jesus' Supper, arrest, betrayal, trial and execution, and resurrection (14:1—16:8).

The foregoing arrangement assumes that the Passion Story had begun with Jesus' arrival in Jerusalem. But Mark was not himself satisfied with that assumption. To discover an earlier pivot in Mark's arrangement of materials we should ask where and when the journey to Jerusalem began. For as Mark understood the matter, Jesus had made his plans to go to the Holy City knowing full well what would happen there. Where then did he start on his way to the Cross? Where did he begin to teach his disciples of his coming rejection? Caesarea Philippi. The way began there (8:27) and ended in Jerusalem. This road is marked by a threefold repetition of his teaching: "the Son of man must suffer" (8:31; 9:31; 10:32). The lesson was prompted by the disciples' recognition that he was God's Messiah (8:29). In this and each successive lesson, the Teacher made clear the fact that the disciples had started walking on the same road. Anyone who follows this Master must take up his own cross (8:34). His interest focused not so much on his own Passion as on theirs. Satan tempted them to expect a more successful leader (8:33), to substitute other standards of greatness (9:35), to set other requirements for entering the Kingdom (10:15), to want glory without shame (10:37). At every point, by precept and example, Jesus sought to correct their evasions, making it as clear as he could that the Son of Man was establishing a new norm of service for every disciple (10:43-45). It must be conceded that Mark included some materials in this section which did not fit this particular theme. He was not inclined to force every episode into arbitrary harmony with his editorial plan. Nevertheless, the basic drift of his thought is clear. He understood this whole section (8:27—10:52) as a necessary prelude to Jesus' death and to the mission of the disciples.

We must constantly remind ourselves that Mark was not writing a biography of Jesus. He was shaping an account of the beginning of the gospel. He was doing this with the materials at hand, anecdotes which came to him through various channels, often without reference to date or place of origin. Those which we have now surveyed he incorporated into a single narrative, all taking place on the way from Caesarea Philippi to Jerusalem, all pointing toward the Passion, all indicating mounting opposition to his work, all illustrating his intention of training the Twelve.

In our analysis of structure, we have dealt with the last half of the Gospel. What may we now say about the organization of the first half? We must say at once that here the ordering of episodes and teachings is not so dependent upon the Passion Story. The ministry of Jesus before Caesarea Philippi does not fall into a single time sequence, nor do the events take place upon a single road. In this section Mark allows earlier collections of memories to retain their separateness. We find, for example, a collection of debates (2:1—3:6) which center on the points at issue between Jesus and the Pharisees; a collection of parables (4:1-34) which coalesce around the character of the Kingdom; and a collection of marvelous deeds (4:35—5:43) which pose the problem in the minds of people: "Who, then, is this man?"

There is no day-by-day diary, no map of Jesus' movements. No one theme dominates. Mark did not write from an outline of topics, but reported diverse samples of teachings and healings which had been preserved either in oral form or in brief written collections.

Even in this first half of the Gospel, however, Mark kept in mind the outcome of the story, and preserved those memories which pointed toward that outcome. For example, the initial account of Jesus' baptism and struggle with Satan gives an understanding of the vocation which would reach its fulfillment on Golgotha. Later on, Jesus makes this connection explicit (10:38). Another signpost can be detected in the references to John's arrest (1:14) and to his execution (6:14-29), which offer striking parallels, and even previews, of Jesus' arrest and death. Again at 2:20 a prediction of that death is given. Yet again Mark shows how the earliest debates between Jesus and the Pharisees led to the plot to destroy him (3:6). His betrayer is identified as early as 3:19. So, too, the rejection of the prophet by his own family appears as harbinger of final rejection by Israel (6:4). In these early chapters, then, we discern no neatly articulated pattern of organization, but we cannot ignore the frequent anticipations of the end of the story, an end which had become for all Christians the true beginning of the gospel about Jesus Christ.

The Shape of the Commentary

In a sense Mark, as we have seen, wrote his book backwards from its end. We, on the other hand, can only read his book forward from the beginning. And we can write a commentary only in that order.

Since our book is designed for modern students of Mark, it must have an outline and follow a definite sequence. As a commentary, the sequence is provided by the order of episodes in Mark. We will not divide the document into separate verses or chapters, inasmuch as those divisions were adopted long after the document appeared, but we will select for the sake of easy reference the separate units of tradition, which we will call episodes, incidents, or pericopes. Then we will arrange into larger cycles these units, which altogether number more than a hundred. The plan for this arrangement is given in the Outline, but we caution each reader: Remember that this is not Mark's outline, but ours, designed purely for the sake of smoothing the way for a fruitful study of the document.

OUTLINE

The Beginning of the Beginning. Mark 1:1-20

The Title (1:1)
The Prophecy (1:2-8)
The Descent of Power (1:9-13)
The Call of Fishermen (1:14-20)

The Power of the Good News. Mark 1:21—3:6

To Cast Out Demons (1:21-28)
To Heal the Sick (1:29-45)
To Forgive Sinners (2:1-17)
To Defy the Righteous (2:18—3:6)

Responses to the Power. Mark 3:7—6:6

Reactions to Jesus' Deeds (3:7-35)
Reactions to Jesus' Word (4:1-34)
The Response of the Twelve (4:35-41)
The Army of Demons (5:1-20)
The Belief of the Unbelieving (5:21-43)
The Unbelief of the Believing (6:1-6)

The Flock and Its Shepherds. Mark 6:7—8:26

The Appointment of Shepherds (6:7-32)
Shepherdless Sheep (6:33-56)
False Shepherds (7:1-23)
Sheep from Other Folds (7:24-37)
Two Kinds of Bread (8:1-21)
A Blind Man Sees (8:22-26)

The Road to Jerusalem. Mark 8:27—10:52

The Coming Confession (8:27—9:1)
The Coming Victory (9:2-13)
Power to Heal (9:14-32)
Proverbs for the Journey (9:33-50)
The Good News and the Law (10:1-31)
The Coming Baptism (10:32-52)

The Temple and the Vineyard. Mark 11:1—13:37

Hosannas at the Gate (11:1-10)
Curses on the Tree (11:11-26)
A Parable Against the Tenants (11:27—12:12)
Traps Set for the Son (12:13—13:2)
A Warning from the Fig Tree (13:3-37)

The End of the Beginning. Mark 14:1—16:8

Three Forecasts (14:1-16)
The Covenant in Blood (14:17-31)
The Night Watch (14:32-52)
The Twin Trials (14:53-72)
Innocent or Guilty? (15:1-15)
The King's Enthronement (15:16-39)
Fear and Trembling (15:40—16:8)

COMMENTARY

The Beginning of the Beginning (1:1-20)

The Title (1:1)

An ancient writer selected for his opening phrase what a modern writer would choose as the title of his book. This opening phrase was selected with great care so that it would fit the contents of the book and suggest the author's objective. Often, therefore, this phrase should be capitalized and boldly separated from the following verses. Such is the case with Mark:

The Beginning of the Gospel of Jesus Christ, the Son of God

Each word here is strategic. A gospel is news, great news. It is news because it tells of something which has happened. It is great because the event has produced so great a change. The greater the change in human affairs, the more urgent the news. It may of course be either bad or good. The better the outlook, the better the news. If it offers power for men's deliverance (Rom. 1:16), then its excellence beggars comparison. This is the force of the term "gospel." This meaning would have been familiar to anyone acquainted with the Scriptures in Mark's day (Isa. 61:1-4).

This news pertained to Jesus in a double way: it was an announcement which he had made, and also a manifesto about him. He was the speaker, and also the one spoken about. Few books incorporate so diverse a collection of materials, yet few have so unwavering a focus. Whatever the situation and whoever the participants, Jesus stands always at the center. Attention shifts from seaside to synagogue to mountain, or from tax collector to leper to centurion, but always Jesus is there.

"Jesus" was a personal name, frequently adopted by Jewish parents for their sons ever since the time of Joshua (the Hebrew form). "Christ" was an uncommon title. What did Mark understand by that title? The answer is by no means certain, even though one of the earliest and simplest Christian confessions was "Jesus is the Christ." Different people meant very different things when they used this title. Jesus himself seldom, if ever, used it (9:41; 12:35; 14:61-62). Those who applied it to him were often misguided in their views (8:29; 15:32). It could be applied to many others (13:21-22). What then did Mark have in mind? In one sense, the best answer is simply to read the entire story and to include as a definition all that Jesus did. We may summarize by saying that, to Mark, the Christ (the Greek translation of the Hebrew "Messiah") is the one whom God has anointed to inaugurate his Kingdom and to serve as King of his people. Through him God has chosen to fulfill his promise of liberty to captives (Isa. 61:1; Luke 4:18). Even so, this remains a formal and theoretical definition until it is defined by the person who accomplishes this deliverance. Jesus himself is the definition, although his definition was so unique and so unexpected that no one really understood his Christhood until after deliverance had been experienced through him. The gospel discloses the drastic changes which were required in men's thinking before they could fully recognize Jesus as the Christ who had come from God.

Mark believed that another title was especially appropriate to this Messiah: "the Son of God." Again we are dealing with a phrase which has had many connotations, a phrase which we think we understand until we try to give an exact equivalent. Again we must listen to the entire story before we trust our definition. Otherwise we might be trapped into adopting popular notions of gods, angels, heroes, and wonder-workers as divine beings, and applying these notions to Jesus. Mark had learned from Jesus how to think of sonship to God. It must be measured by doing work which God has assigned (1:38), by complete obedience to God's will (3:34-35), by exercising God's liberating power, even through death (2:5; 15:39). The Son is known by his love for the Father and the Father's love for him (1:11; 9:7).

One other expression in the book's title requires comment: "the beginning." We should probably not think of this as if the author were saying: "Here begins my story" or "Here begins the lesson." Just as the term "gospel" did not refer here to the written document (the Gospel of Mark), but to the great message which Jesus and his disciples proclaimed, so, too, its beginning cannot be limited to verse one of chapter one. Does Mark refer to the first episode in the story, that is, the preaching of John and the descent of the Spirit on Jesus? Yes, but far more than this. As we have stressed in the Introduction, Mark considered the entire series of events as "the beginning," everything which led up to the proclamation of the gospel by the Apostles. The point where he ended his story was the point where the Apostles began to shout their

personal testimony that this crucified Man had now been revealed
as the Messiah. In this sense Mark may have wished to remind his
readers of that other Genesis: "In the beginning God created the
heavens and the earth." God had begun a new thing in creating a
new humanity, yes, even a new heaven and a new earth (Rev.
21:1). Understood against this background, Mark's title makes a
tremendous assertion.

The Prophecy (1:2-8)

It was the custom of Apostles in Mark's day to include in their
witness to Jesus the assurance that through him God had carried
out his promises. Such an assurance was much more than an incidental matter, for unless God is faithful he is not truly God. When
he acts he must act in harmony with previous covenants. He had
earlier bound himself by firm oaths to his people, the Israel of the
Covenant. Those promises, in turn, had served as the basis for the
work of all the prophets. Through Malachi, God had pledged to
send a "messenger of the covenant" to prepare the way. He had
warned men that this messenger would burn "like a refiner's fire."
Preparation required purification, a purification involving both
soap and fire (Mal. 3:1-4). Through the prophet of the Exile,
God had announced to Jerusalem the boon of wars ended and
iniquities pardoned. He had indicated that a highway would be
constructed in the wilderness. One sign of this revolution would
be a crying voice (Isa. 40:1-5). Those messages, delivered
through the prophets, had demanded of Israel both dread and
hope, both stringent repentance and humble expectancy.

For Mark the appearance of John as God's messenger constituted a first and strategic step in the fulfillment of such promises.
John was this voice in the wilderness, sent to make straight the
paths of the Lord. Israel must heed his commands as the commands of God himself.

Why must this happen in the wilderness, with its nomadic dress
and its meager diet? To symbolize the sharp break with the institutions and culture of the city, to dramatize the renunciation required of those who would accept his authority, to intimate that
this prophet who came in the "spirit and power" of Elijah (Luke
1:17; Mark 9:13) was to protest against the complacency and the
idolatry of the accepted religious leaders. An authentic and ancient prophet had appeared again, the signal for a divine account-
ing with God's people, the omen of a shift in the course of history.

Why the voice? John's strategic preparation of the road for the Messiah lay in his preaching. About what did he preach? The other New Testament books give a fuller account than does Mark's Gospel (see Luke 3:4-17). God's judgment was near at hand, as close as the ax to the root of the tree when the woodsmen have marked it for felling. The crisis was such that no one dared rely on his parentage, his piety, his prestige. Everyone faced God's awesome winnowing in which the chaff would be burned. Everyone needed forgiveness; apart from forgiveness no one could survive. Those who recognized this situation (and this would include all who accepted John's authority as a prophet) joined in humbling themselves before God.

Why this baptism? John not only spoke but acted. His action was itself a dramatic sign of the new day, a sign in which both the prophet and the people declared their faith. Multitudes came from great distances to confess their guilt and to throw themselves on God's mercy, praying for the day of redemption. Their journey to the Jordan showed their willingness to leave the old world and its entangled complicities, and to plunge into the fires of God's righteous judgment. More than this, it was a symbolic repetition of that earlier crossing of the Jordan under the leadership of Joshua, when God had led into the Promised Land those emigrants who were ready to venture all on his leading. Now again God was calling for a new decision and was opening up a new Land of Promise. John established the Jordan as the frontier between old and new. Those who crossed this frontier were pledging themselves to place God's will above all earthly securities and ambitions. When they descended together into the water, this was no conventional gesture, but a radical self-renunciation and an equally radical reliance on God. They sought to cross the boundary between a cursed past and a blessed future. When Paul spoke of baptism as being "buried" with Christ, he showed how radical was this act (Rom. 6:3-4). But John's demand on those who heard him preach was no less rigorous and ruthless. This baptism of repentance for the forgiveness of sins was nothing casual or trivial; it was sober and revolutionary. Otherwise Jesus would not have reckoned it as the work of the promised Elijah.

John not only demanded humility; he demonstrated it as well. He knew that he was himself unworthy of the new day. He had been sent from God only to prepare his people for it, to lead them to its dawn. Both he and they would need something more than

forgiveness for the past; they would need to be baptized by the
Holy Spirit, who alone could give them power and life. But because John's authority came from God, their forgiveness also
came from God. Together they were leveling a new road, looking
toward a "mightier" one who would baptize with the awesome gift
of the Holy Spirit. So Mark saw prophecy fulfilled in the mission
of John. His Roman readers would likewise see in John's baptism
the essential beginning of their own baptism, their own forgiveness, and their own preparation to receive the Lord.

The Descent of Power (1:9-13)

"In those days" is a strange way of dating so important an
event. Mark was not concerned with the exact year or month; in
all likelihood he did not know it. He was more concerned with
showing how God had linked the vocation of Jesus to that of
John. In this he followed the accent of the Apostles' sermons,
which often began by appealing to "the baptism which John
preached" (Acts 10:37). Those were the days when God had prepared Israel for the coming judgment, when Israel itself had been
called into the path of revolution.

The statement that "Jesus came from Nazareth of Galilee" is
remarkably brief. It identifies Jesus' home town and, since the
town was small and little known, his home province also. But
Mark shows no interest in Jesus' earlier life in Nazareth, no interest in his training or home. Jesus made the long trip, presumably on foot, though Mark says nothing about the manner of the
pilgrimage. He simply assumes that Jesus had heard what John
was doing.

Nothing is said about Jesus' state of mind. He simply came and
was baptized, along with others who had answered John's call. To
Mark there was no difficulty in supposing that Jesus shared with
his fellows the baptism of repentance, the will to turn away from
the past and to face toward the coming Judgment. But when Jesus
was baptized, all heaven—yes, and all hell too—broke loose.
Mark declares that three things happened, each of which he de-
scribes very tersely and very symbolically.

1. "The heavens opened . . . the Spirit descending." By "heavens," Mark was speaking of more than the sky. "Heaven" is the
biblical way of referring to the invisible throne of God, the source
of God's mysterious words and deeds. A view of opened heavens
enabled a prophet to glimpse God's decisions and to grasp God's

purposes for men. The man to whom the heavens are unveiled receives the gift of prophecy and the authority to speak in God's name (11:30-31). This is the significance, too, of the Spirit which descended like a dove on Jesus. We are not asked to visualize this dove, but to meditate upon earlier deeds of the Spirit and earlier descents of the dove. Mark's account echoes the story of divine creation in Genesis when the Spirit had brooded over the waters (Gen. 1:2). It thus connotes the faith that again God had released a mighty creation force. The symbolism is also reminiscent of the story of the great deluge, when the dove had brought glad tidings to Noah (Gen. 8). Reflecting for centuries upon such episodes, Israel had come to expect that the New Age in human affairs would be inaugurated by the Spirit's descent. The Spirit would convey heavenly grace and power to the Messiah (Luke 4:18-21) and through him bring peace and joy to men. Water, dove, wilderness, Spirit—all these images suggested agelong struggle and elicited great hopes. Where the dove descends, there God's power begins again to operate.

2. "A voice came from heaven." The voice put into words, powerful words taken from Scripture, God's address to Jesus: "Thou art my beloved Son." In being baptized by John, Jesus was baptized by God's Spirit and appointed to do God's work as God's Son. What is the precise weight of these words? We cannot be entirely certain. They echo phrases in the Second Psalm (2:7) and in the prophecy of Isaiah (42:1). The echo of the Psalm intimates that God was now crowning a King on his holy mountain who was destined to inherit and to rule all the peoples on earth. The echo of Isaiah intimates that God was now calling a Servant through whose suffering justice and peace would be restored to a dark and tormented world. It was thus intimated that Jesus' mission would embody the authority and power of a world ruler in the atoning love of a world servant. We will find that successive episodes illustrate this same fusion of the regal authority of a king with the gentle humility of a slave.

3. "The Spirit . . . drove him . . . into the wilderness." Mark closely connects the descent of power with what at first sight seems its antithesis. For what is the first sign of sonship? Struggle. The Spirit who had anointed Christ as Son immediately "drove him" (the Greek verb is a harsh one) into the wilderness. From the first the path of sonship would be lonely and desolate, for this required him to do battle with Satan, the ruler of darkness. This

battle must proceed without aid from men. It must proceed even within the stronghold of the Devil himself: "the wilderness . . . the wild beasts." (For an instructive parallel, read Revelation 12.) The work of both John and Jesus sent them to this territory of the Enemy. With the aid of the Spirit, Jesus vanquished the Tempter, and that victory assured triumph in temptations and battles which were to follow. But Mark leaves little doubt in the reader's mind that the struggle was genuine and long. The "forty days" calls to mind the deluge in Noah's day (Gen. 7:17), the wandering of Israel in the wilderness (Deut. 29:5), and Elijah's period of wrestling with his call (I Kings 19:4-8). After this victory Jesus was qualified to wrest other men from Satan's grasp. He could now command the demons and they would recognize his authority. The descent of power from God had thus precipitated a challenge to the only other ultimate power-center in human affairs and had accomplished a victory which could be extended far beyond the original beachhead.

What are the connections between this story and the life of the Church in Mark's day? The main links are clear. The Church as a whole, including every believer within it, was baptized by the same Spirit. All were reborn from above, from heaven. Their sonship, as brothers of the Son of Man, was acknowledged by God. Moreover, they were made sons for a purpose, chosen to carry out a redemptive mission. Their call to serve men was everywhere dependent upon Jesus' power as God's beloved Son. They were struggling daily with the same Tempter in the same wilderness (Rev. 12:14; Heb. 3:8-10). The memory of Jesus' baptism was therefore more important than the memory of their own, because his baptism had preceded and included their own.

The Call of Fishermen (1:14-20)

The episodes in Mark are so loosely linked together that it is quite impossible to recover the length of the time intervals. How long a time elapsed between Jesus' battle with Satan and his return to Galilee? We do not know. The duration of the private battle was not a matter of dates on the calendar. What seemed important to Mark was the fact that it was only after his anointing with the Spirit and his victory over Satan that Jesus could take up his public work. One other event intervened—the arrest of John. This must have posed its own form of temptation to Jesus. Was it not evidence of the folly of the expectation which John had held?

Did not this public hostility and government brutality prove the futility of such dreams? If Jesus continued to proclaim joyful tidings, could he expect any more merciful fate? Instead of frightening Jesus from his work, however, this arrest struck the signal for which Jesus was waiting. He took over John's message and carried it even into Galilee, the very stronghold of Herodian power.

We do not have a full transcript of his opening message. Mark gives us a summary in a single sentence, each word of which calls for expansion. Of what "time" did Jesus speak as being "fulfilled"? The time of sin and sorrow, the time of patient waiting and penitent preparation, the time of crucial decision and risk, the time which God had determined and promised, the time when he would bring final judgment and mercy to the earth. Of this fulfillment, the preaching and arrest of John were tokens, as were Jesus' struggles in the wilderness. God had declared war on Satan's empire, and Satan had responded with all-out mobilization of his forces. God had set his Kingdom in motion. It was now coming toward earth from heaven. It was pressing in at the very doors. Signs of its nearness might be detected in the descent of the Spirit and the triumph over the Tempter. Another sign was simply the presence of Jesus himself with his authorized manifesto. As surely as he was God's Son, so surely was his announcement God's own declaration. God's impending judgment was indeed as terrifying as John had indicated. "Who can stand when he appears? For he is like a refiner's fire" (Mal. 3:2). But the judgment must be so caustic just because the redemption was so great. Apart from God's word, there could be no peace. If forgiveness were to be final, repentance must be total. Only when men became free from the past could they become open to God's future. This was what gave to Jesus' call a double thrust: "Repent, and believe in the gospel." All that Jesus taught was simply an expansion of this keynote sentence.

Note, for example, how the double word "repent . . . believe" was immediately matched by the double deed of leaving and following. The summoning of men to join him was an essential part of Jesus' vocation, a part which he undertook at once. The first who "left . . . and followed" were four fishermen. In describing their response, Mark gave only a glimpse of what originally must have been a much longer episode. This quartet may well have been disciples of John and recipients of his baptism (John 1:35).

They probably had met Jesus on earlier occasions. They almost
certainly had heard Jesus give at greater length his proclamation.
But the miracle lies in the fact that they had accepted it: Is the
time fulfilled? Yes. Must we "repent, and believe"? Yes. Symbolically the story stressed two things about these men. First, they
had abruptly and completely broken away from the routines of
their job and from the securities of their home. Second, Jesus had
pledged to teach them how to fish for men. All the later episodes
in Mark's document make clear how Jesus had redeemed this
pledge, as one "lesson" followed another. At the end of their
"course" these first four had in fact become fishermen. The initial
story, therefore, reminded every Christian reader of the intended
outcome of his own decision to leave and to follow.

The story of the call of this quartet also suggested to early readers that Jesus had begun his task of creating the Church at the
very outset. He had been sent for the very purpose of fishing for
a community of fishermen. In these five Galileans the later Church
was foreshadowed. In what happened one could see mirrored how
the Messiah makes his "catch" in every situation: a call, a com-
panionship, a sacrifice, a shared task. It is not surprising that in
early Christian art the Church was pictured by the rough sketch of
a boat, with fishermen at their nets.

Thus with great economy of words Mark suggested the beginning of the beginning: the prophecy and the prophet, the baptism
with water and the Spirit, the struggle with Satan and the triumph
of God's Anointed, the proclaiming of the news and men's double
response, the call and commissioning of the Apostles, the emerg-
ence of the Church, the journey together into Capernaum.

The Power of the Good News (1:21—3:6)

In the opening paragraphs of his book Mark had introduced
Jesus of Nazareth as a prophet who had received authority from
God as the Messiah. The announcement of how the time had been
fulfilled, along with the summoning of the four fishermen, had
been the first public clue to the Messiah's authority. God's power
had now to be released publicly, but without losing its heavenly
depth. Disclosure would not dispel its mystery. Each exercise of
this power, as Jesus followed step by step the leading of his unique
vocation, would intensify the question, "What is happening here?"
(see 1:27). The presence of power was undeniable; not so its

origin. In the succeeding episodes, the disciples watched with increasing surprise the results of this power as it now operated among men.

To Cast Out Demons (1:21-28)

The site of Jesus' earliest ministry was the province of Galilee, still an important governmental division in modern Israel. The site of the first invitation to discipleship was the lake, still the location of a substantial fishing industry. On the northern shore of the lake was a bustling city, Capernaum. Excavating the ruins of the third-century city, archaeologists have uncovered a large stone synagogue and a Roman-style forum, buildings which indicate an active community. Nearby was the place where fish were salted for export. In this city lived the first disciples (1:29), and here much of Jesus' earliest work was carried on.

"On the sabbath he entered the synagogue." It was probably a large building, with many of the citizens in attendance. Every week they gathered to hear the Scriptures read and interpreted, to pray for daily strength, and to praise the God of Israel. Here the scribes expounded the lesson and taught the people what God's Word meant for them. Here, then, Jesus appeared among the scribes as one of the teachers. But immediately the manner of his teaching created astonishment. Whereas the other scribes relied upon the authority of the Scriptures and of their tradition, this visitor spoke as a prophet, relaying a message straight from heaven and acting as if he had been assigned to speak in God's own name.

Mark did not pause to tell how long, on that first occasion, Jesus spoke and what he talked about. Mark had already given the gist (1:15). Presumably Jesus spoke of the new opportunities which God had made available for fishermen and for housewives. He made clear the threat which God's action posed for the powers of the Devil; he issued God's offer of freedom and peace. Whatever he may have said, one response paralleled the response to his baptism. There the descent of the Spirit had been recognized and resisted by the Devil (1:13). Here the authority of the Spirit was recognized and resisted by the demons, who were, so to speak, private soldiers in Satan's army. An unclean spirit (or a demon) discerned that this strange preacher was "the Holy One of God." He rightly inferred that God had sent Jesus to "destroy" them. He realized that the Holy One would allow no compromise: "What have you to do with us . . . ?" Satan himself had learned

this lesson in the wilderness (Matt. 4:1-11). Now Jesus demonstrated his authority over Satan by commanding the demon to de-
part from the man. The demon obeyed his new master and, after
one final display of his anger, released his prey. News was made
in that synagogue that day, even the ordinary kind of news. Rumors raced throughout the countryside. Inevitably men asked,
"What is this?" What can explain this thing? A man had appeared
with a message concerning God's power. He had spoken a simple,
direct word, and strong chains had parted.

It is not surprising that the story, wherever it is read, creates
similar reverberations. Of course in that day the belief in demons,
in the reality of their power over men and the possibility of ex-
orcizing them—all this was taken for granted. Other men had
been known for their ability to ban these unwelcome spirits. Even
today the phenomenon is by no means as rare as most of us suppose. From a good friend I have heard a similar story of how she,
a pastor, evicted a demon from a man on the island of Truk. In
Mark's day, of course, such an incident was more common. As
Mark told the story for Roman disciples, it was just one example
of how the power of the gospel could free men from many de-
spairs which constricted their hearts and destroyed their health.
Jesus' word still exerted in Rome its mysterious power to produce
surprise and awe, expectancy and fear, wonderment and uncer-
tainty. Public curiosity and personal interest in being healed, in
Rome as in Capernaum, combined to raise the question: By
what authority? To that question each of Mark's readers had to
provide his own answer.

To Heal the Sick (1:29-45)

Such notoriety and excitement can easily mushroom, especially
if other startling things happen in close succession. Such was the
case on this particular Sabbath. The group of five men went to
Simon's home for lunch. There the hostess was in bed "with a
fever." Jesus "lifted her up . . . and she served them." The terseness of this story baffles both the interpreter and the reader. Why
did Mark not say more? We do not know. But we can surmise why
he says what he does if we remember that this anecdote speaks
of the home of disciples, a home in which a member of the family
was sick. In similar homes in Rome, disciples would be conscious
of the Lord's abiding presence. They would tell him of "her."
And this Lord would come, would take "her" by the hand and

would lift "her" up. Then she would be healed and, since she might not have been a believer, would now become one who "served." This is a picture of how the servant Messiah made servants of those whom he blessed with his presence.

Sundown in Israel marked the end of the Sabbath. Men could again walk and work freely. The unexpected presence of a divine healer created a furor. So the crowds gathered in front of the house, bringing with them the sick and the tormented. Mark summarized what happened most tersely: "and he healed many . . . and cast out many demons." The two episodes just recounted were only a selection of many such stories that might have been told.

One feature of this summary calls for comment. In freeing man from demons Jesus bound the demons to a pact of silence, "because they knew him." Why did Jesus do this? Why does Mark mention it, here as well as later in his narrative? (for example, 3:12). Did Mark add this detail in order to explain why men had not recognized Jesus as the Messiah during his lifetime? Some interpreters think so. Or did Jesus want to discourage the misleading notoriety and confusion which would result from open publication of these wonders? Possibly. A premature popularity might have forced him into a type of "headline" ministry which would have defeated his purpose. Or was he aware that a faith produced by the spectacular and the abnormal, a faith based on popular gossip of what Jesus had done to someone else, would always be inadequate to support believers through the trials of ignominy and death which true faith entailed? (4:16-17). Mark is reticent about disclosing Jesus' motives, but he sees great significance in the fact that the demons recognized in Jesus "the finger of God" (Luke 11:15-22). They realized that with the coming of the Kingdom their own days were numbered. Mark also implies that the onlookers, who did not understand the mysteries of the unseen world as the demons did, were unaware as yet of the true source of Jesus' power.

The silencing of the demons is thoroughly consistent with the fact that Jesus immediately chose to slip away from the crowd, avoiding further clamor and excitement (1:35). He would not allow the crowd to deflect him from his major work. He was a courier with news which must be broadcast as widely and as quickly as he could manage it. The news included, to be sure, the power to evict demons; but if he permitted the hubbub which was produced by this power to deflect attention from God's commis-

sion, he would forfeit his assignment. Time and again during the
weeks which followed, he had to keep his heart focused on the
basic purpose: "why I came" (1:38). Time and again concentration on this single task led him to withdraw into the wilderness.
(The Greek word translated "a lonely place" is the same as that
rendered "wilderness" in 1:3 and 1:12.) This place, symbolizing
the ministry of John and the trial of Jesus by Satan, was the place
where by prayer Jesus could himself resist the attractions of popularity, where he could renew his dependence on God, and where
he could return to his initial commission. The disciples were as
surprised by his desire for seclusion (vs. 37) as by his power over
evil, yet Mark knew that these two were linked together.

Try as he did to evade the spectacle-hungry crowds, however,
Jesus could not escape the claims of human helplessness. "A leper
came to him" begging for help, confident that Jesus could cleanse
him. Then, as now, leprosy was a major scourge. Leprosy was
more than a physical malady, for it made one a social derelict,
unable to live in any settled community, unable to touch anything
or anyone without spreading the awful contagion. A leper became
a religious outcast, cut off from synagogue and Temple. Wherever
he went he was met by the horrible shudder, "Unclean." Shunned
by the whole world, hating and despising himself, he lived within
a frightful shell of uncleanness and hopelessness. This particular
leper, however, had not given up all hope in God's power and
compassion, for he came to Jesus with his pathetic cry. The Messiah was moved with pity. He touched the untouchable and thus
took upon himself the dreaded contamination. He commanded,
and the leprosy departed (the language of verse 42 suggests that
Jesus was expelling an unclean spirit). He commanded again, and
the leper went to the priest for that certificate of cleanness which
would restore access to the homes and hearts of his neighbors.
Although the Messiah commanded the leper to conceal who had
cleansed him, his command could not be obeyed. Word of what
had happened spread so widely that Jesus again had difficulty in
avoiding publicity. In Jesus' work as master of maladies a light
shone which could not be totally hid; for it made too obvious a
difference to the sick, the insane, and the leprous. The next episode shows how the power to cleanse and to heal was inseparable from the power to release men from the paralyzing effects
of guilt.

To Forgive Sinners (2:1-17)

Back again in Capernaum, the city which may have become his home, Jesus' main activity was "preaching the word." Much is left unsaid about this "word" because Mark's readers knew its basic content—God's disclosure of his plan, of his Kingdom and its coming, of the threat of condemnation and the possibility of blessedness. The "word" simply meant the gospel (4:33). Now this "word" became embodied in a strange action. When four men came carrying their paralyzed friend, the word of God's mercy became a very special word to this particular individual: "My son, your sins are forgiven." Such an assurance that his guilt was cancelled tore this man loose from his paralysis. The twisted mind in the twisted body was healed, and he returned home to take up his customary duties.

It was not strange that the word embodied in such a deed should have created resistance. But the scribes objected not to the cure of paralysis but to the forgiveness of sin. "Who can forgive sins but God alone?" For a man to claim God's power was blasphemy—that is, unless God had actually invested him with his own power to cancel sin. The complaint of the scribes was used to underscore the important issue: Was this act of forgiveness genuinely God's work, or not? If not, Jesus was rightly labelled a blasphemer. But if this forgiveness, obviously effective, was truly from God, then the basic "word" of Jesus was also true: "The kingdom of God is at hand" (1:15). This, in fact, was the key issue in everything that Jesus was to do. In raising their question the scribes were undoubtedly sincere. Moreover, if their negative answer were correct, they were fully justified in uncovering the fraud. Their hostility was in some ways more natural than the faith of the five friends. Nevertheless, the experience of the five supported a more positive answer: the gift of forgiveness and health was, in fact, a gift from God. Their amazement led them to glorify God.

The core of this story, therefore, should be located in the power-laden word of Jesus: "My son, your sins are forgiven." We should notice the address. Why should Jesus have said "My son"? Did the Son of God, authorized to speak for God, take this way of declaring that this paralytic was in fact God's child, welcomed into God's family? And was this welcome as a son equivalent to the cancellation of his sins, similar to the way in which the father welcomed the prodigal in Luke 15? Whether or not this is so, we can be sure that to Mark the fact that God had forgiven this man was a way of declaring that God had opened his Kingdom to such sinners. By telling this anecdote, Mark was conveying the very message to his readers which according to Luke was delivered in the synagogue at Nazareth (Luke 4:16-19). Mark, however, was content to picture all this in his staccato accounts of Jesus' healings. Both Mark and Luke understood these events as signaling "the acceptable year of the Lord."

From synagogue to house to seaside—Jesus seemed to move as the mood struck him. He did not limit his work to any favored setting. But whether in one place or another "he taught." Everywhere he found "the crowd" waiting to hear him. He did not in advance determine whom he would seek out. Men of the most diverse occupations met him; selection of followers seemed both unplanned and coincidental. Now it is Levi sitting in his office. Levi was a tax collector and was therefore detested. He made his living by taking money from his countrymen in order to give it to the foreign imperialist. Moreover, no person who tried to fulfill all the Mosaic requirements of purity could collect taxes. Only a Jew who craved money more than respectability or righteousness could accept such a job. We can imagine, then, the public outcry at Jesus' dramatic gesture, for he summoned such a man to be a disciple. He welcomed him into the Kingdom. He accepted entertainment in Levi's home, and this of course meant that they ate together. To eat together meant that they would be bound by the mutual covenant of brotherhood, with all its obligations. This was extremely offensive to the scribes, because the whole company at the table was a degraded lot. Levi was only one of the many sinners who had been welcomed to that table. The scribes could not avoid asking why. The answer of Jesus condensed his vocation into a single spear thrust which was to be remembered wherever the gospel was preached: "I came not to call the righteous, but sinners." Levi was as much in need of a physician as the leper and the paralytic had been. On his sickness and his sin, Jesus and the scribes agreed; that was why the scribes could not understand the behavior of Jesus and his disciples. Their conduct was just as obnoxious as their message: that God would send such a Messiah to call such people into such a kingdom (Rom. 5:6-11).

To Defy the Righteous (2:18—3:6)

Each of these stories indicates a cleavage between Jesus and "the scribes of the Pharisees" (2:16). Slowly but steadily this conflict sharpened. Whatever Jesus did upset conventional patterns of behavior, defied the current codes of duty, and placed God in the position of condoning sin by forgiving the sinner. The "scribes" were those ministers of the synagogue who were charged by vows to defend the Scriptures, to teach the people to obey the Law, and to protest against willful defiance of Israel's Covenant with God. They looked forward to the coming of God's Kingdom, but they knew that when that time came God would decisively punish all sinners and reward all the righteous. Accordingly, anyone who condoned sin must be attacked, all the more if he did this in God's name. When Jesus persisted in ignoring the Law, they were duty-bound to defend the Law against such treason.

The Pharisees illustrated their devotion to God by fasting. John's disciples also believed that to prepare for God's Judgment Day sinners must mourn for their guilt. Jesus' disciples, by contrast, celebrated the approach of the new order by feasting and drinking in the most dubious company. Why? "Ours is a wedding feast," was the reply. "We are guests of the bridegroom himself. Here he is with us. Who can mourn at such a time?" When this debate (vss. 18-20) is seen as the sequel of the previous banquet (vss. 16-17), it becomes clear that to Mark the wedding feast was recognized as a symbol of the joys to be shared in God's Kingdom. As the bridegroom, the Messiah includes his Church in those joys. This Church is made up of sinners whom he has accepted and who can do nothing less than rejoice over their forgiveness. To attempt to confine their joy within the restrictions required for mourning would be as foolish as to pour new wine into old wineskins. For those who believed, the news of God's forgiveness had changed everything (1:14-15). Like the paralytic and the tax collector they entered into a new friendship, where they lived in the exuberance of a new hope. For them only the happiest of celebrations was appropriate. To act with the old gloom and fear, to carry out the old practices, even to obey the Law designed for the earlier day—all this would have denied the truth and would actually have destroyed the "old wineskins." But of course the Pharisees had no inkling that this rejoicing could be justified. For them there should be no wedding feast until the great transformation was visible to all. They were, in fact, the guardians of what Jesus called the "old wineskins." And among the most cherished of these wineskins was God's command to keep the Sabbath Day holy. They were therefore bound to challenge this teacher with regard to his defiance of God's rules for the Sabbath.

The Christians in Rome, to whom Mark was writing, were at odds among themselves over whether or not they must hallow the Sabbath. Some disciples treated all days alike, while others insisted that the seventh day of the week (the Sabbath, our Saturday) was holier than other days (Rom. 14:1-7). The dispute produced keen animosities. The Sabbatarians condemned the others and were in turn despised by them. As a result, the two factions found it virtually impossible to worship together, for they could not agree on the time for meeting. In such a situation this story about Jesus (vss. 23-28) was cherished by the "liberal" group, and Mark was one of their spokesmen. The story made clear that Jesus not only "broke" the Sabbath in the synagogue itself, but also broke it by walking farther than the law of the Sabbath permitted and by encouraging his disciples to do forbidden work. It was forbidden to work by harvesting grain and husking it for food. When the defenders of the Sabbath protested, which was nothing less than their duty, Jesus did not deny the infraction. He appealed to the precedent of David, of whom the Messiah was Son (see I Sam. 21:1-6). More important, he appealed to the principle of creation. Who made the Sabbath? God. If so, then God's Son should be superior to the Sabbath, for he is its Lord. (This again was outright blasphemy.) For whom was the Sabbath made? Man. Then the conditions of God's New Creation (the Son of Man with his people) justified a new understanding of the Sabbath. The Son of David and his friends should be as free as David and the priests had been. The dawning of the New Age had produced a revolution. Jesus was showing how this revolution affected the institutions designed for the Old Age, including even God's Law. Since the Pharisees could not accept the revolution, they were bound to defend the old. Their conflict with Jesus measured the incompatibility of the new and the old. Here began the later enmity between the Church and the synagogue.

Now the Pharisees must watch Jesus for other infractions, for every infraction would increase the damage to law and order. They must be ready to challenge this rebel at every opportunity. And virtually every episode provoked such an opportunity, because Jesus with his disciples acted with what must have seemed to be reckless freedom. If a man needed healing, they did not wait until the next day, when it would be entirely legal to heal. They provided the help at once. To postpone the healing would, in their eyes, make the Sabbath an instrument for doing harm, even of killing (3:4). The Messiah came not to observe holy days but to save life. Each act of mercy was a demonstration of the truth that salvation makes all days holy, because every day presents its opportunity to heal and to free. Only the hardness of men's hearts can blind them to this true holiness.

Yet as guardians of the holy, the Pharisees saw no other course than to destroy the cause of such blasphemy, such defiance of God's Word. Because they needed the help of political authorities, they held a committee meeting with the supporters of Herod, seeking the surest ways. As ambassador of the new "law and order," Jesus had no other option but anger at the Pharisees, combined with grief over their blindness. For the issue was not merely whether to break or to obey the Sabbath law, but whether to reject or to believe the message that God's power had been released for man's healing.

Responses to the Power (3:7—6:6)

We have now arrived in the story at a point where the conflict has taken the sharp outlines of black versus white. The Pharisees, Sadducees, and Herodians are so obsessed by Jesus' threat to the Law that they must seek to destroy him. He and his disciples withdraw to the lakeside, followed by crowds with a different obsession. The enmity is clear-cut. But Mark was too sensitive to the intermediate shadings in human responses to be content with the sharp cleavage of men into two camps. So he gives us a collection of episodes which suggest the more complex patterns of action and reaction.

The alert reader will discover at this point also a change in the form of the episodes. From 1:21 through 3:6 we have a cycle of stories which probably circulated orally as a collection before Mark incorporated them into his document. Sometimes these anecdotes are called "pronouncement stories" because each story is told for the sake of the climactic pronouncement of Jesus. The story in 2:15-16, for example, makes clear the meaning of the saying in 2:17. Sometimes these are called "paradigms," because they set forth patterns of behavior which the Apostles wanted their hearers to imitate. Sometimes they are called "controversies" because they recount debates between Jesus and the scribes and thus illustrate the superiority of the Christian arguments against the synagogue.

From 3:7 through 6:6, however, these forms of tradition are absent. Rather we find a collection of parables (4:1-34), and then a collection of miraculous signs, including the quieting of the squall and several amazing cures. These stories are told with great detail, and with less concern for the sayings of Jesus. At the outset of these two collections we find four rather heterogeneous summaries (3:7-35): a summary of popular excitement; of the names of the Twelve; of the reasons for scribal rejection; and of the character of his followers. In these paragraphs Mark distinguishes four quite different reactions to Jesus' deeds.

Reactions to Jesus' Deeds (3:7-35)

First there is the anonymous multitude, drawn by gossip, fascinated by the excitement, coming from all directions and with various motives. They want to get as close as possible to this worker of marvels. They want souvenirs of these unusual happenings. Some of them, harassed by illness, are pathetically eager to touch this migrant healer before he leaves their vicinity. Strangely disturbed by his words, bewildered by his power, they guess only dimly the scope of what is happening.

Then there were the unclean spirits, active in the excitement, permeating the sick minds and divided hearts. Their confession was wrung from them unwillingly, "You are the Son of God." Unfortunately for these unclean spirits, the confession was a true one. Satan believes in God and trembles; so, too, his soldiers believe in God's Son and tremble (James 2:19). They know that his power can muzzle them, and even expel them from their lodgings in human souls. Nevertheless, even though in this case they knew that they had been bested, they kept up their battle for those lodgings. In all this there was an uncanny contrast between the demons' response and men's. The demons understood what was happening; they had no illusions on that score, but they feared it. The crowds did not understand; they had numerous illusions, and yet they welcomed what was happening. The demons, having closer contact with the invisible aspect of reality, could discern the truth. Men, having greater dependence on the visible, were confused by it. Even so, the Messiah ordered the demons not to share their knowledge with men. Men must find out the truth for themselves; they could not profit from faith unless it were their own. At this point the faith of the demons was more intelligent than that of the crowds of followers.

From this larger company of followers, Jesus had chosen twelve. At this point Mark gives us the roster of names (3:13-19). The place of the disciples' commissioning was significant—a mountain. In ancient oriental thought heaven and earth came nearest to each other on a mountaintop. The mountain was the place most appropriate for especially sacred revelations (9:2; 13:3), for significant appointments, for bestowals of grace and power. This was no casual or routine rendezvous. The Messiah had created a unique group for special duties. He had taken the initiative in selecting them, not because of their desires or capacities, but because of his plans for them.

"He appointed twelve." The number was intentional. Jesus wanted new representatives of the twelve tribes of Israel. In a sense these men were to become the patriarchs of a new Israel. This appointment anticipated the later promise that they would sit on thrones, ruling the tribes (Matt. 19:28). The thrones were set around his throne, symbol of a shared authority. But this authority stemmed from his gift and training. For the time being they were to be "with him," learning the mysteries of God's new order. Then they would be "sent out" as Jesus' own delegates to the world, exercising his power to preach and to heal. He gave them new names, surnames, to signify this new role. Appointment, however, did not guarantee faithfulness. Even in this small number there was one "who betrayed him."

There is much that escapes us if we read this naming of the Twelve without considering the Scriptures on which Mark and his readers had fed their minds. For example, Isaiah 43 should be carefully studied in this connection. In both passages, the Lord is creating Jacob and forming Israel, calling them by name because they belong to him (Isa. 43:1). He promises to be with them when they pass through the waters (vs. 14; compare Isa. 43:2 and Mark 4:35-41). He promises to gather sons and daughters from the end of the earth (Isa. 43:6), for they are to be his witnesses, his servants (Isa. 43:10). Yet in the time of Jesus, as of the prophet, the salvation of God was rejected by the people "who are blind, yet have eyes" (Isa. 43:8).

In Mark, this blindness is bluntly described (3:20-23). Yes, Jesus had been able to release men from demonic obsessions. But his friends took this as a sign of mental disease on Jesus' part. And the scribes explained it by saying that he was himself under the power of Beelzebul, the prince of demons. Privates in the demon army were bound to obey the commands of their chief, even when the chief had shared his authority with a man like Jesus. To put it in military terms: Beelzebul was the commander-in-chief of this army, and Jesus had been made his general.

Jesus gave a twofold answer. While admitting that Satan can order his soldiers to do various nefarious tasks, it is incredible that Satan should cast out his own soldiers from his own realm. He would not thus be a party to weakening his own kingdom. That in itself would be suicide for the Prince of Evil, and suicide is not to be expected of Beelzebul. This was the negative reply. On the positive side, the Pharisaic charge could not be correct if as a result of Jesus' authority men were actually being released from slavery to evil spirits. The Pharisees did not deny that certain men had been so released.

The second and positive answer is hidden in the parable of the Strong Man (vs. 27). The "strong man" represents Satan. "His house" stands for a man or a society which is demon-possessed. "His goods" refers to Satan's right and delight in ownership. Anyone who would contest Satan's ownership, who would take from him or from the men or the society under his control, must first bind Satan himself. And that, by implication, is just what Jesus had done. He had wrestled with this strong man and had overcome him (1:12-13). This alone explained why he had been able to "plunder his house." It was because God had first bested Satan that Jesus had been able to exorcize demons and to endow his Apostles with the same power (3:15). This power, far from being demonic, was actual proof that God was at last evicting Satan from his home within men and their society.

Because this truth was so basic, Jesus supported it with a most stern declaration: sins and blasphemies of all kinds may be forgiven, but it is unforgivable to call the Holy Spirit an "unclean spirit." Centuries of exegesis have not established the precise meaning of this warning. We may not be far wrong if we say that to call the Holy Spirit "unclean" is to deny that the Holy Spirit has power to overcome the Devil. It is a flat denial that God can forgive sins. It is an absolute form of despair, for a person thereby rejects in advance the possibility that men can ever be freed from bondage to evil powers. In this despair, a person actually gives to Satan the status of Almighty Father. Such despair cannot be forgiven, because it bolts the only door by which forgiveness may enter. This, in fact, was Satan's objective—so to blind men that they would think of the works of the Holy Spirit as unclean. They would then reject Jesus and later reject the Apostles (13:9-13), for it was Jesus' intention in naming the Apostles to give men through the Apostles freedom from Satan (3:15).

During these early weeks of Jesus' ministry, people had been compelled to ask, "Who is this man?" Now he asked them, "Who is my family?" The two questions were linked together. Furthermore, just as the first question could be answered in two different ways—a tool of God or a tool of Satan—so also the second question. Was not Jesus' family obviously made up of his mother, brothers, sisters? And were they not unsympathetic with his work? Here they came calling him, trying to draw him back home to more normal life. (Verse 31 may continue the thought of verse 21.) Jesus' reply appeared to repudiate them entirely. "Here are my mother and my brothers!" Here men were rejoicing over the news of the Kingdom, men who had accepted forgiveness and healing. Quite naturally and spontaneously they were feasting together. By accepting God's invitation and obeying it they had become more closely bound to Jesus than his own kin. In fact, they had become his very own family.

There is much more to this incident than the casual reader will notice. Behind the incident lay a revolution. In Jewish circles, much more than elsewhere, a man's primary obligation was to his family "according to the flesh." To reject one's duties to his parents was to flout God's commandment. Why, then, did Jesus do as he did? Because the dawning of God's Kingdom had produced a new kind of kinship. Those who welcomed this gift became *his* brothers, and he became *their* brother. The sign of this new community was common obedience to God's will, common joy over God's forgiveness, common freedom from the Devil, a common task in proclaiming the Kingdom of God.

As Mark understood this episode, he saw here a clear picture of the Church. He even saw in this story a picture of the early house-churches of Rome, a group of disciples gathered in a house, sitting with Jesus in their presence, listening for him to reveal the will of God, and ready to obey it, regardless of opposition from

families, friends, and Pharisees. As Mark saw it, Jesus had promised to every disciple a new family, and through the Church he
had fulfilled that promise (see 10:28-30). The Messiah was not a
distant king, ruling the world from a distant throne. He had
chosen to dwell among simple folk in their home, sharing with
them his authority and his love. The only requirement for entering his family was obedience to the God whose work he was
doing. God—his Kingdom—his Messiah—the Twelve—the Messiah's family—such was the line of progression by which the revolution was taking hold of things.

These various snapshots thus give a composite picture of the
varying reactions to the dawning of the Kingdom: bitter and
deadly hostility by the religious leaders, grudging and fearful respect by the demons, amazed and confused wonder by the crowds,
baffled and mistaken concern by brothers and friends, partial acceptance of authority by the Twelve, humble receptiveness and
joy by his new family. This same range of reactions is reflected in
Mark's selection of a cycle of parables as an interlude in his drama.

Reactions to Jesus' Word (4:1-34)

As we read the first of the parables and its explanation (4:1-20)
we note the various circles of listeners. The Twelve form the
smallest circle. A bit larger is the circle of the Twelve with "those
who were about him" (vs. 10). This circle represents all the disciples of Jesus, which in Mark's own day would be the members
of the churches. The largest circle included these groups plus all
who heard his preaching without making a decision about it (vs.
1). Again we may suppose that Mark had his eye on the Roman
situation, with its combination of listeners, believers, and leaders.

The parable was given to all (vss. 1-9); the explanation was
given only to those who had chosen to follow, for only they would
have experienced the hazards (vss. 14-20). We should therefore
read these two sections as if they were placed in parallel columns.
"The sower sows the word" (vss. 3, 14). This farmer is quite obviously Jesus, whose word is the message of God's Kingdom with
his power to heal and to bless, and with his call for pilgrims. (For
other appearances of "the word" with this inclusive reference, see
4:33; 2:2; 8:38.) We should remember of course that in Mark's
day it was the Apostles (3:14) who sowed the word, that is,
preached the gospel.

"Some seed fell along the path . . . when they hear, Satan immediately comes and takes away the word" (vss. 4, 15). Now in addition to Jesus and his message, our minds are forced to deal with certain believers (symbolized by the type of soil) and with Satan (the birds). Thus the window opens into the hearts of disciples in every generation. And this window is not very different from the glimpse into Jesus' heart at the time when he had received the word, that is, when he had been baptized. He had been called, had joined the company of penitents, had received the Spirit, had been declared God's Son, had been assigned a task. Satan had immediately come and had tried to snatch the word from Jesus' heart. But he had failed. Jesus had repelled him by his determination to live by God's will alone (Matt. 4:4). But with Jesus' disciples the story often had a different ending. Although they had shared in the same call, the same baptism, they almost immediately succumbed to Satan's taunts and wiles. From the first the prospect of discipleship had filled them with dread, not joy. The first sign of opposition unnerved them. They were quite unable to relay the word to others, for Satan's word proved more persuasive.

The message of the Kingdom had also fallen on rocky ground (vss. 5-6, 16-17). Here the drama lasts longer, but it is no less tragic. It has three acts: I. The response of joy because of the exhilarating sense of peace and freedom; II. Momentary endurance with deceptive signs of strength and growth; III. Defeat because of persecution. Men had accepted the gospel, but the external pressures combined with inner weakness have resulted in apostasy. Christians needed no further elaboration of this picture (13:9-13).

Then there was the brier patch (vss. 7, 18-19). Here the Enemy employed subversive tactics: division within the heart of the believers. Joy over forgiveness competed with anxieties over earthly security. Desire for the Kingdom competed with "delight in riches." Contrary ambitions choked the word. How could a believer relay Jesus' news to others while he was worried at every step over the unavoidable risks? In his work the seed would produce no grain for a new sowing. In this case the defeat might be very subtle, in fact, so subtle that a disciple might be quite unaware that his faith was fruitless, but the defeat was genuine nonetheless. A disciple cannot preach the Kingdom while he is inwardly loath to make sacrifices.

The parable, however, reaches its climax in its fourth stage: the good soil (vss. 8, 20). Here the accent falls on the assurance that the gospel achieves its purpose in those disciples, however few, who "hear . . . accept . . . and bear fruit." The harvest is abundant, despite the failures of much of the sowing. This harvest, in turn, takes the form of new seed for sowing. The mission which Jesus had received from God would thus be continued successfully by the mission which the Twelve received from Jesus. There was little in the parable, thus explained, to baffle the mind of Roman disciples, if we recall the situation in which they lived.

Nevertheless those disciples were often baffled, if not by the meaning of the parable, at least by the situation which they faced. Considering the obstacles to preaching the gospel in Rome, their responsibility to relay the word was not easily discharged. In the other parables of Jesus, Mark spoke to them in this bafflement. Why, for example, should there be such deafness to the word when it was spoken to "those outside"? The answer was contained in a tiny riddle (vss. 10-12). This riddle speaks of two groups, the outsiders and the insiders. What determines their location? Their response to the announcement of God's invitation. The outsiders "hear but [do] not understand." They have ears but no comprehension (vs. 9). Such deafness to God's voice cannot be taken as proof that the word itself is false or that the messenger is a fraud. The ultimate reason for the deafness is hidden in the mystery of God's purpose. Men can never explain why some believe and others are deaf, but they can trust in God, nevertheless.

But this fact in turn raised problems for the messengers. If outsiders are so deaf, is it not the part of wisdom to stop sowing the word so widely? Should they not limit the news to those who are eager to receive it? To such a protest Jesus applied several pithy proverbs. Do you light a lamp and then cover it with a box? No more should you restrict your work of delivering God's message. It is intended for all. If some prove to be blind, that is God's business, not yours. If they do not have hearing ears, you never will know it except by speaking to them. And you, you disciples who have received the message, the measure of *your* hearing depends upon the measure of your giving (vs. 24). Unless you relay the news, you yourselves will lose what has been given to you. Your own powers of hearing will grow to the degree that you boldly set the light of the Kingdom on its proper stand (vss. 21-25).

Another question often mounted to the minds of those disciples who proclaimed the message as fearlessly as Paul, and who yet found only a scanty harvest, far less than even the thirtyfold of the parable. How should they respond to such discouragement? Two parables were relevant to this dilemma. The first (vss. 26-29) was a reminder that not even the best farmer can control the growth of the grain. "The earth produces of itself" while the farmer goes about his work, confident that the grain will grow and that there will be a harvest. Men should not fret over a disappointing prospect. God takes responsibility for that.

The final parable in this cluster (vss. 30-32) taught disciples that just as the largest shrubs grow from the tiniest seeds, so the final results of sowing the word should not be judged by the initial size of the seed. Disciples will be fooled completely if they judge by the inconspicuous beginnings of their sowing. God has already assured ample harvest. (Similar attitudes toward the work of sowing the message of the Kingdom were expressed by Paul in I Corinthians 3:5-9.)

To Mark, this manner of teaching was typical of Jesus. Some parables by their nature would convey no meaning to non-disciples. But they had profound meanings for disciples who had ears for detecting their explanation (vss. 33-34).

The Response of the Twelve (4:35-41)

Even the Twelve, however, were hard of hearing, and Mark may have found some consolation in that fact. They had been close to Jesus. He had named them the patriarchs of the New Israel (3:13-19). They had heard him explain why and how the word fell so often on thorny or rocky ground. Yet they themselves proved to be soil as hard and unyielding as that. When tribulation and persecution had struck (vss. 16-17), their own joy had evaporated and their endurance had failed. Panic had quickly driven peace from their hearts.

Such a situation is reflected vividly in the story of how the disciples reacted to sudden storms. This story had no doubt been told and retold on many occasions before Mark embodied it in writing as a sequel to the parables. By the time it reached him, the story had itself become something of a parable. The central characters are of course Jesus and his disciples, the disciples of A.D. 70 in Rome as much as those of A.D. 28 in Galilee. Jesus' rebuke and assurance were as real to the former as to the latter, for his presence was as real now as then. Various items in the story reveal these parabolic overtones. The boat, for example, had become one of the symbols suggestive of the Church. The sea also had its con-

ventional meaning as the realm of evil, under the control of the
Devil, and therefore the source of hostility to the Church. The
storm expressed all the conflicts which can befall the Church,
especially those involving violent persecution, as under Nero in
the Rome of A.D. 64. We should notice that the decisive moments
in the story are provided by the dialogue. "Do you not care if we
perish?" Such a wail may well have been the cry of dereliction of
many (Rev. 6:9-11). Disciples were often less concerned about
Jesus' work than about their own fate. They expected him to care
for them because their danger had resulted from their association
with him. "Peace! Be still! . . . Why are you afraid?" If we think
of the command as addressed to the wind and the waves, then it
recalls the way in which Jesus had ordered the demons to silence,
for demons were believed to be active in the sea. But the command did not ignore the disciples. The demons working in their
hearts had replaced trust with frenzy. Jesus' control over wind
and sea (the hostile world) simultaneously exerted control over
the disciples' fears of death.

Told with such accents in mind, the story evoked in each disciple's mind the hazards of his own life and the fact of his own dependence on Jesus for courage. To have Jesus "on board" did not
enable him to escape storms; it carried him to the eye of the hur-
ricanes. Literal shipwreck was not, of course, excluded (Acts 27).
But more common were such storms as public ridicule, social
ostracism, economic boycott, lynching parties, judicial trials (for
a sample list see II Cor. 11:23-28). To know that Jesus had power
over *this* kind of storm was more urgent than to know that he was
fully able to quiet other kinds. But this knowledge could not be
secured in advance. Storms must be faced by his followers on
their own. They must be subjected to the terror of helplessness.
Only then would they appeal to Jesus, but even then his first word
would be a stern rebuke: "Cowards all." Even so, his rebuke
would help to quell their hysteria. He had power which they could
appreciate only at their wits' end. The Messiah who thus spoke
through this story to the Christians of Rome was a Lord who had
conquered death and who could therefore deliver men from the
fear of death (Heb. 2:15). In reading this story they might be
led to say: "We can now face death unafraid because he has
triumphed over it."

A story like this indicates that Christians had come to view Jesus' salvation in figures taken from the Old Testament, where the

same salvation had been granted by the same God. The story about Jesus fulfilled the word of God to Israel: "Fear not, for I have redeemed you . . . When you pass through the waters I will be with you . . . I love you . . . I am the LORD, and besides me there is no savior" (Isa. 43). The same theme has been captured by numerous hymns, and these hymns are often simply modern versions of the ancient Psalms with which Jesus and Mark had praised God (Pss. 65:7; 107:23-32).

Such a line of exposition will not completely satisfy the reader. Various details in the story resist reduction to symbolic images. Why, for example, are the other boats with him? (vs. 36). Why did they take him "just as he was"? Why should the cushion on the stern seat be mentioned? Is it significant that it was evening? Perhaps no single explanation can explain all these items equally well. Some readers may feel that to interpret the story as a "parable" is too easy a way of escaping a hard problem: Could Jesus thus command the wind and the sea? This protest may be justified. Yet which is a harder problem: the intellectual problem of believing in Jesus' control over nature, or the personal problem of risking death in line of duty? For the Roman Christian, the latter problem was primary. Can I face death on account of Christ and accept it unafraid? The story in effect says, "Yes, if Christ is with you in the boat, meeting the eye of the same hurricane." But the story also says that even the Apostles at first failed to trust his power.

The Army of Demons (5:1-20)

Again we meet "a man with an unclean spirit," this time in a story which is told with great relish and at great length. As background for this contest we recall several points. Jesus had demonstrated his Messiahship by his successful struggle with Satan, his control over demons proving the reality of God's Kingdom. The casting out of demons had also been evidence of the forgiveness of sin and the social reconciliation of men. When Jesus had authorized the Twelve to proclaim the good news, he had given them power over demons. But their alarm at the storm had proved their unreadiness to use this power. They were still dependent on Jesus to overcome their enemies. He had been able to exorcize the demons in the wind and the waves, but not they. Now they are confronted with a case of a man as storm-tossed by the demons as the disciples' boat had been.

The diagnosis is detailed. The man is clearly insane. He has broken away from contact with normal society; he lives in the cemetery, contaminated by his contact with the graves. He resists all efforts to restrain him, breaking chains with superhuman energy. Night and day he disturbs others with his shrieking and damages himself in self-torture. So diverse are his actions, so strong his delirium, that the demon's name is fittingly called Legion. As there were 6,000 men in a Roman legion, there was a comparable contingent of demons in this man.

The conversation between Jesus and this demonic multitude is fascinating. The man met Jesus as he came out of the boat. In fact, so eager was he to meet Jesus that he ran. The man even worshiped Jesus. He was unable to escape the Legion, but he clearly wanted to escape. Jesus responded to the man's eagerness by commanding Legion to get out. Legion protested in effect, "Let me alone . . . We have nothing in common." Jesus would not grant such a petition. He gave notice that he was about to expel the Legion. Recognizing Jesus' intention, Legion at the last moment proposed a compromise. If he must be cheated of a human lodging, he preferred to inhabit swine rather than to migrate from the country. Jesus accepted the bargain. To the swine the demons were to go. As the sequel shows, there were enough demons in the one man to drive 2,000 swine crazy. In this climax we may detect sharp satire. Though the demons get their request, the joke is on them, because this residence leads to the dramatic death of the swine, with the result that the demons themselves return to the sea, that agelong home of the Devil, which Christ had already overcome in the previous episode.

In this highly developed account it is difficult to detect profound theological or moral values. It was told with gusto for its own sake, because it suggested what terror shook the demonic army when the Messiah began to use his power to free men from their fears and frenzies. Like other wonder stories, this one could easily arouse doubts. Did it really happen? The story itself provides a triple attestation. There is the word of the herdsmen, bemoaning their loss. There is the surprise of those who had known this man before and after his healing (vs. 15). And there is the report by those who had seen the curious happening. We might expect that this episode would bring a huge increase in the number of followers, or a crusade to have Jesus extend his stay in this place. Quite the contrary. Men "were afraid." That is, they them-

selves were far from being immune to the demons. Exactly like
the Legion, they wanted to win safety from eviction by increasing
their distance from Jesus (5:17; compare vs. 7). Only the man
who had been healed, it seems, was grateful. He wanted to ac-
company Jesus. We might expect Jesus to welcome him into the
ranks of disciples. Jesus commanded him rather to go home to
his friends and tell others about the new gift of health.

The Belief of the Unbelieving (5:21-43)

Mark now turns to a double story in which two separate incidents have been telescoped into one. For purposes of interpretation we may separate the two. Both episodes present difficulties to
the modern reader, who is bound to raise dozens of questions
which cannot be answered with assurance because of the absence
of evidence. We cannot be certain at many points, nor should we
claim greater confidence than we possess. We shall be content if
we can understand why Mark wanted his Roman audience to
know these stories.

The first story tells of Jairus. Jairus was a Jew, of course, who
had been chosen as president by the board of elders in the synagogue. His office would be of special interest to Mark's readers
because in all likelihood Christians had found such leaders obsti-
nate in their opposition to believers, especially if they supported
Mark's attitudes toward the Law (see the comment on 2:1—3:6).
"Surely a person of such importance from among our enemies
could not become a Christian," they might say. The tradition,
however, tells of just such a person who had been impelled to
come to Jesus for help when his daughter was dying. Had he allowed the debates over the Law to keep him away from the Master when emergency struck? Not at all. He had shown his reverence for Jesus by falling at his feet. He wanted health and life for
his daughter, and therefore he wanted Jesus to bless her. But there
had been a delay, a delay which increased the tension, because the
girl died before Jesus could arrive. Surely now the trip would be
futile. The Teacher might be able to heal, but not to restore life.
Jairus should cancel his request. But Jesus acted as if the death of
the child had not changed the situation. The initiative passed from
a man seeking help to a Lord seeking to give help. He ordered Jairus to replace his fear with faith. He limited his entourage to the
three disciples whom he wanted to train in the saving of life.
When he heard the women keening over the death, he told them

to stop wailing as if there were no hope. He spoke with authority to the girl, "Stand up." Then he forbade people to talk about what he had done. At every point they were amazed—and so is each reader. Why is the story told in this fashion? Why is nothing said later on about the girl, or her father, or the neighbors?

The only actors who reappear later are Jesus and his three disciples. Mark's readers were especially interested in them. Peter, James, and John had been there. What had they learned? That Jesus had shown compassion for a potential or real enemy. That he had disclosed his power over death. That this power was not to be publicized (vs. 43) until after his own resurrection from the dead. That people should be helped even though they had not joined the Church. These are among the possible implications of the story for Roman Christians. They should be willing to do as the three Apostles had done: to go with Jesus to such a home, to proclaim there a Master who had triumphed over death, to carry his compassion wherever there was genuine mourning.

As in other stories, the expositor must confess that no single set of comments is adequate to explain the text. The narrators of this incident took for granted the power of Jesus over death and life. They assumed that a proper posture before this Lord was to prostrate oneself. They themselves had known how the hands of Jesus could bless, how his word could raise the dead. They naturally associated his power with that of Old Testament heroes (I Kings 17:17-24; II Kings 4:32-37). They recalled how Jesus had commissioned the Apostles to "raise the dead" (Matt. 10:8), and they had heard accounts of how this commission had been carried out (Acts 9:40). Also they knew how easy it was for weeping to give way to laughing (Mark 5:38, 40), but how difficult for fear to give way to faith.

The second story (vss. 25-34), an interlude in the first, tells of an unknown woman whose twelve-year illness had proved the helplessness of other physicians, had left her penniless and defenseless. Her illness, a continuing hemorrhage, had extended the period of ritual uncleanness for twelve years (Lev. 15:25-27). But she had not become hopeless. The excitement over Jesus had revived her spirit. She touched his robe and was healed instantaneously. Some stories would have ended there, but not this one. A strange dialogue ensued between Jesus and his disciples. Jesus, aware that "power had gone forth from him," wanted to know who had received it. His disciples in effect said, "The crowd is too

large to find out. How can you expect us to know such things?"
What would Mark's readers think of this? Disciples should know
when people have been healed by the Lord's power. There follow
the closing words between Jesus and the woman. On her part
there was a humble confession of her secret "theft." On his part
there was a benediction, the sort of benediction which Christians
had heard and which it was their duty to use in similar cases of
need: "Daughter, your faith has made you well; go in peace, and
be healed of your disease." Thus both of these stories show how
frequently Jesus found faith where his disciples had expected
nothing but unbelief. Like him, Christians should minister not to
the well but to the sick (2:17). They should sow the word even
on the least likely soil (4:4-7). A sense of desperate need is often
the occasion of faith among the outsiders.

The Unbelief of the Believing (6:1-6)

The reverse is also true. The Master frequently found unbelief
where others might expect to find faith. The story of Jesus' home-
coming in Nazareth remained a vivid example of this. The Messiah came to his own synagogue on the Sabbath Day. Those who
joined him in worship were of his own house and kin. They knew
the mighty works which he had done, of which the preceding
chapters are reminders. They recognized that his teaching spelled
out a wisdom most surprising. They did not deny that amazing
things had been happening. Their trouble came from another direction: they knew him too well. They knew his mother, his sisters, his brothers; there was nothing unusual about them. They
knew his trade; nothing striking there. They could not fathom how
a man from their own village had been given such wisdom and
power. They could not believe in him as God's anointed prophet.
They could honor him as a fellow citizen, but not as a prophet
with the power of the New Age. They were offended by the claim
that one of themselves could have received divine work to do. No
more than the Pharisees could they explain his words or acts as
authorized by God rather than by Beelzebul. It was at their unbelief that Jesus marveled, in contrast to the marvelous faith of the
unclean woman (vs. 6; 5:34).

We should not leave this anecdote without commenting on the
report it gives concerning the household in Nazareth of which Jesus was a member. A modern reader is grateful for the names of
Jesus' brothers. But he is even more surprised that nothing more

is said about them. Mark was not interested in them as persons, nor in their impressions of Jesus, nor in the life of this particular household. They are viewed only as background for this scene. They are mentioned only to show that Jesus was too ordinary a man for people to expect marvels from him. There is irony in the question—which we cannot overlook. Even so, the irony carries valuable incidental information.

"Is not this the carpenter . . . ?" Here is the only clue in Scripture to Jesus' occupation. And even this was dropped out of some manuscripts, presumably because copyists thought such a reference beneath the dignity of their Lord. Other manuscripts, perhaps for the same reason, change the form of the question: "Is not this the carpenter's son?" The very reason which made later Christians hesitate to think of the Lord as a carpenter had been present, in reverse logic, among the people of Nazareth. They were not ready to think of this carpenter as the Lord. In other words, both believers and unbelievers have found it extremely difficult to understand how Jesus could be at once fully man and fully God.

What more is said about Jesus' kin? If we read "carpenter's son," we should assume that Joseph was alive. If we read "the carpenter," we would naturally infer that Joseph had died before Jesus' prophetic career. It is possible, of course, to argue that Mark does not mention Joseph lest he contradict the story of the Virgin Birth. This argument does not convince many readers, in part because these words were spoken by Nazareth residents who would not have known, and in part because they speak of the brothers and sisters without any suggestion that as such they were not fully and normally related to Jesus. Mark's lack of interest in these brothers and sisters is characteristic of the Church of his day. None of the sisters and only one of the brothers appears later in the New Testament. This one is James, who became a follower of Jesus much later, perhaps after the Resurrection, and who for a while was considered an Apostle and a leader in the Christian community in Jerusalem (see I Cor. 15:7; Gal. 2:9-12; Acts 15:13-29). The sisters of Jesus get no further mention in the New Testament. To Mark it was enough to know that Jesus was rejected by his family, that his townsmen looked down on him because of his humble connections, and that Jesus himself had chosen a new set of mothers, sisters, and brothers (3:35).

The Flock and Its Shepherds (6:7—8:26)

In compiling this section of his book, Mark again used a collection of materials so diverse that it is almost impossible to discern a common theme, an unbroken thread of action, or a continuing intention. The title we have rather arbitrarily chosen is suggested by 6:34. The choice will seem less arbitrary when we notice the central emphasis upon the two feedings of the flock (6:33-44; 8:1-21), and when we realize how flexible are the biblical ways of referring to the flock. Elsewhere in the Bible the needs of the sheep are variously seen as hunger, danger, lostness, sickness, and suffering from derelict shepherds. Elsewhere, too, their salvation depends wholly on God's provision of shepherds, whose authority and teaching, whose compassion and care, will meet their diverse needs. Mark inherited an extensive vocabulary concerning shepherds and their flocks, and he applied it freely to Jesus as the True Shepherd, to the Apostles as his undershepherds, and to the false shepherds who contested the right of leadership. We will understand this vocabulary more clearly if we first read other key biblical passages (Pss. 23; 77; 78; 80; Jer. 23; Ezek. 34; Zech. 7-14; Luke 15; John 10; 21; I Peter 5).

The Appointment of Shepherds (6:7-32)

"He called to him the twelve." By this carefully accented number, Jesus emphasized their work as the new patriarchs of the flock of Israel; like Jacob of old he was establishing them and their tribes to receive his blessing and to continue his Covenant (see Gen. 49). "He . . . began to send them out." Earlier Jesus had called them to be "with him" (3:14); now he did what he had intended from the beginning—he sent them out as his messengers to continue and to extend his own work. They went out "two by two," rather than as a group, in order to reach more villages. They went out in pairs rather than singly, because in Jewish custom every promise needed two witnesses (Deut. 17:6), and these messengers were to give testimony not only to the word of God but also to the response of the towns (vs. 11). They carried Jesus' own authority over sickness and over demons (vss. 7, 13).

The urgency of their journey was implied in the command to travel light. They should not tarry long in any town. Only one thing were they allowed to carry: "a staff." Was this staff a walking stick, to symbolize pilgrimage? More likely, it was a rod or

crook, symbol of the shepherd's work (see Rev. 2:27; 12:5; 19:
15). The same word, however, was used for the king's scepter, the
mace which gave him power to govern (Heb. 1:8). The shepherd
and the king—these were the two basic symbols of Israel's government, since the days of David. The scepter and the staff—these
belonged to the shepherd-king. It was the authority and the compassion of Jesus which the Apostles exercised.

They were to take "no bread, no bag, no money." The Master
was insistent on this (see Matt. 10:9-10; Luke 10:4). They were
not to take thought for the morrow, what they should eat or wear
(Matt. 6:25-34). They would need no insurance for the future;
baggage would only hamper their movements. They had much to
give and therefore appeared as penniless suppliants, dependent on
whatever hospitality might be offered, for the character of their
wealth would be made more conspicuous by their poverty (II Cor.
8:9). Their claims on men's hospitality must reside wholly in their
preaching and healing (6:12-13).

In our culture, where abundance is the rule and penury the exception, this luggage of the disciples seems curious indeed. What
instructions could be more damaging to public relations? Yet we
must take this picture as accurate not only for this single journey
of the Twelve, but also for the regular practice of Jesus (who had
"nowhere to lay his head"), and for the traveling evangelists of
Mark's day. It is likely that Mark and Peter had gone together on
their trips with precisely this kind of equipment. The Apostles
knew that such weakness and poverty were effective means of proclaiming that men should repent (I Cor. 2:3-5).

The reader who wishes immediately to see what happened on
the Apostles' trip is rudely interrupted by a strange story about
John the Baptist, a story which fits better after 5:43. Let us look
then at this story. It was introduced by discussions concerning Jesus. Who was this newscaster? Three possibilities were given:
John the Baptizer, Elijah, another of the ancient prophets. (We
shall comment on these a bit later when these three are mentioned
again in 8:27-30.) Is Jesus to be thought of as John? If so, then he
is John "raised from the dead," for John had already been executed at Herod's command. This mention of John prompts Mark
to include at this point a popular tradition concerning his martyrdom. The text gives the story so fully that we need add very little.

Why should Mark have included this bit of gruesome material in his message concerning Jesus? A certain answer is not

available, but we may suggest a few possibilities. For example, we note several tantalizing parallels. Jesus had begun his active work only after John had been jailed (1:14); now his Apostles begin their active work only after John's death. In both cases the reference to John gives a preview of the fate of the others. Jesus had just bestowed the gift of his Kingdom and his power, to the end that men might be healed. King Herod bestows a similar gift (vs. 23), and it is used in spiteful vengeance to secure a prophet's death. The banquet of King Herod in the palace offers the sharpest contrast to the banquet of King Jesus in the wilderness (vss. 39-44) Because of the link between the ministry of John and Jesus (9:11-13; 11:30), the rejection of John runs parallel to the rejection of Jesus (6:1-6). More significantly, this "passion story" of John shares many traits in common with the later Passion of Jesus. King Herod and King Pilate fill similar roles. Both are hesitant to do the deed. Both want to evade responsibility. Both consent to issue the death warrant only in order to please others. Both assign the unwelcome task to soldiers. In both stories there is interest in the burial; in both there is report of resurrection; in both the recollection of Elijah is prominent. Whether or not Mark was conscious of these parallels, he believed that both John and Jesus had served the same gospel, and that the work of both would be established in God's Kingdom.

Shepherdless Sheep (6:33-56)

When the Shepherd had begun his ministry, the public clamor aroused by his teaching and healing had forced him to withdraw to the desert for prayer and rest, and for a renewed understanding of his mission (1:35-39). Now after the undershepherds had been pursuing the same task of teaching and healing, and had aroused similar excitements, they too needed the desert, and the reminder of their central purpose (6:30-32). On this occasion, however, the crowds anticipated their "retreat" and waited for them in the desert. The sheep were there, without a shepherd. Who would help them?

Obviously Mark and his readers knew the answer. Jesus was the Shepherd who had compassion, and he showed this compassion first of all by teaching the throngs about God and his Kingdom. This teaching was essential to the shepherding of Israel. Then came the hunger and the need for food. At this point the story takes a surprising turn, for now Jesus expected his disciples to provide the food. Had he not appointed them to teach and to heal? Had they not been able to do many things by his authority, by the scepter of his Kingdom? "You [who are in training as God's shepherds] give them something to eat." That sounded like a plausible request. But had Jesus, and had the disciples, forgotten his earlier commands? He had just ordered them to take no money and no bread (6:8). They must have been fully justified, therefore, in protesting that they themselves could not be expected to raise "forty dollars," or to have enough food in their bags. How could Jesus rightly ask such things of them? Certainly he must have known that they had too little food even for themselves (vs. 38). The expectation of Jesus was manifestly unfair unless from the first the story had been couched in figurative language. It was not unfair if Jesus had in mind "the bread of life," "the food which endures to eternal life," if he thought of food as the act of accomplishing God's work (John 6:27, 28, 35). It was not unfair if Jesus wanted to show how Israel can truly be fed not from bulging granaries but from loving concern (John 21).

Almost all interpreters of this story find its values not on the surface but beneath it. There one finds important linkages to many other biblical episodes and teachings. The story echoes the account of God's gift of manna to Israel in the wilderness (Exod. 16). It runs parallel to stories of Elijah and Elisha (I Kings 17:8-16; II Kings 4:42-44). It is shaped according to expectations of the great banquet which would be celebrated in the Messianic Age. It is associated with the Eucharistic meals in the churches of Mark's day, and the account of the Last Supper (14:17-25). It is a fulfillment of Psalm 23 (the shepherd, green pastures, still waters, the table, the enemies), and of the petition for bread in the Lord's Prayer. When we read the narratives with these associations in mind we will glimpse the multiple meanings of many key phrases: "he looked up to heaven" (the home of the Shepherd-God, the one from whom Jesus had been sent, and to whom he will return); "he . . . blessed, and broke the loaves" (thanksgiving, sanctification, fellowship, Covenant vows, suffering); "he . . . gave them to the disciples to set before the people" (the Apostles are deacons of the Church, who must receive the power from Jesus before they can feed the sheep); "twelve baskets full" (the disciples who began with almost no resources ended with a vast surplus for each; to feed God's flock, God would provide whatever was needed).

In summary we may confess that the story staggers us with its wealth of meanings. It can itself feed five thousand and yet leave much of its reservoir untapped. We do great injustice to such a story if we reduce its purpose to a single point or a single doctrine. No notice is given in the story itself to any special amazement over what had happened. "And they all ate and were satisfied." Nothing is said to indicate that anyone marveled at this. In fact, later comments prove that the mere production of bushels of food was not the point of the story in Mark's mind (6:52; 8:14-21). He was much more aware of the truth that before Jesus' death the Apostles had been unable to feed God's flock, the truth that this ability had in fact come to them after Jesus' death, and the truth that this later capacity had resulted from Jesus' act, when he had blessed the bread and had broken it (6:41; 14:22). Mark knew that this breaking of the bread had been accomplished in the breaking of Jesus' body, and that the broken body must be eaten by those who hunger and thirst for righteousness (Matt. 5:6). Thus this text, like many others, draws its ultimate glory from the disclosure of God's grace in the death of his Son.

After the supper together in the wilderness, Jesus sent his disciples away, for obviously they needed further experience before they could become shepherds. He dismissed the crowds, an act of blessing and benediction similar to the closing word after the observance of the Supper in the Church. Then he went to the mountain again for prayer. He and the Twelve were separated, he on the mountain and they in the boat on the lake (the Church in a hostile world). He could see them, and know their distress; they did not dream of his presence, for even when he came near, they thought they were seeing a phantom. He found no obstacle in wind or waves; they were unable to make headway. When they saw him, the disciples were at first more terrified by this apparition than by the storms, until he commanded, "Take heart." But when he had joined them in the boat the winds and the fears were stilled.

The episode surprises us with its ending: "they did not under-, stand about the loaves." Presumably Mark is saying that if the Twelve had understood the loaves they would not have been bewildered by Jesus' coming to their boat. The two stories, therefore, are linked together. If the meaning of one is grasped, the other should be clear. "But their hearts were hardened"—this phrase in the New Testament refers to a particular kind of spiritual blindness. Men are thus afflicted who are unable to see God's glory or to receive his freedom (II Cor. 3:14). So also are those who in hearing the gospel are blinded to its truth (John 12:40). Another example is the Pharisee who in loyalty to the Sabbath rejected Jesus' emancipating power (Mark 3:5). In this passage the Twelve are blind to the presence of God and to his care for men. This suggests that his appearance to them in the storm center was really the manifestation of God's saving power. (The phrase "It is I" is the same phrase as the distinctive name of God in Exodus 3: 14.) The encountering of storms by the Apostles (and later on, by the Church) is thus seen to be a part of God's plan when he commands the Church to take to the boats in order to prove his presence to them in the crises of their journey. This "lesson," then, is the same as that taught by the story of the wilderness supper. The loaves prove the power of the Lord (Ps. 23) to sustain and to nourish his people in all situations. But the disciples did not understand this, nor did they understand that the Messiah was seeking to use the wilderness and the tempest to teach them how to feed his sheep and to triumph over their adversities. Such a lesson must have been as reassuring to Roman Christians after Nero's purge as to the Twelve in Galilee. "It is I; have no fear." But such a word could not penetrate hardened hearts.

What happened when they landed provided a stark contrast. The sick people rushed to be healed because they "recognized him," whereas the Twelve had been terrified by his presence in the storm. As he had fed his sheep, as he had saved them from the deeps, so now he heals them. That is his work. But the Twelve are still blinded to the full glory of the revelation of God "in the face of Christ" (II Cor. 4:6).

False Shepherds (7:1-23)

When Jesus had compared the crowds who came to hear him to sheep without a shepherd (6:34), he had implied that Israel as God's flock needed shepherds and that those who had been thus appointed had been derelict in their duty. It was but a short step to think of the scribes and Pharisees as shepherds who had become hirelings, or even thieves (John 10:1-13). This sharp contrast is implied in this scene, when immediately after Jesus has fed the sheep in green pastures the pseudo-shepherds attack him on the basis of the food laws of the Pentateuch. Their devotion to their traditions had induced them to ignore the needs of the flock.

The explanation of these traditions (vss. 3-4) is rightly placed in parentheses, for this is obviously an editorial comment which would not have been needed in Galilee by a Jewish audience. It is a footnote which shows that Mark was writing for many Gentile readers who would not otherwise have understood the Jewish customs. To help such readers Mark gave comments of this sort, making him one of the earliest commentators on the gospel. He was of course preceded by many commentators on the Jewish Scriptures. "The tradition of the elders" was in fact the result of efforts by sincere, devoted scholars to interpret the Law (Lev. 22:1-16) in such a way as to guide laymen into obedience to it. God himself had said, "You shall be holy; for I the LORD your God am holy" (Lev. 19:2). The Pharisees sought to define this holiness and then to teach men how to become holy.

The first point at issue stemmed from the complaint that Jesus' disciples ate with hands that had not been cleaned from the impurities of Gentile market places. (Mark was more concerned about Roman disciples than about Galileans.) Jesus defended his disciples by a stinging charge against their defamers. They were double-talkers, honoring God verbally, worshiping him in gesture, but far from understanding his will. They had not, in fact, defended God's commandment but had replaced it. This commandment is not something that can be read and then obeyed mechanically, but a living will which can be understood only when the heart is animated by the same purpose (vss. 6-8).

The second point grew out of this critique, and had no direct bearing on the washing of hands. Jesus gave one of many possible examples of how particular scribal rulings had become means of evading explicit written commandments. Take such a commandment as the honoring of parents by their children (vs. 10; Exod. 20:12; 21:17; Lev. 19:3; 20:9). The scribal ruling seems to have been this: If a son had made a vow to offer to God, or to the Temple, property which was later needed to support his parents, he should give to this vow priority over his family obligation. The scribes were aware of the conflict of duties, but their decision seemed to Jesus to stultify the weightier duty, and to determine the issue not by the desires of a heart close to God's purpose but by an impersonal and legalistic appraisal of obligations.

A third point, far more inclusive and radical, dealt with the question of the source of uncleanness (vss. 14-23). Here Jesus discussed not the problem of the washing of hands or pots but the problem of how to determine what is clean and what is unclean. No longer is the basis for judgment to be found in the written Law but in Jesus' new law. Like Moses from Sinai, he "called the people to him." This edict was intended for all of them, and he uttered it with great authority: "Hear me." It was an edict, and yet it was a parable (vs. 17). It was a parable because it required a special understanding, which he expected only from disciples but failed to get: "The things which come out of a man are what defile him."

The new law thus promulgated was not a written law, to be sure, for the point of reference was the heart. Nothing which does not enter the heart can defile a person. Food does not enter the heart, therefore it cannot make one unclean. But what comes from the heart, this and this alone is decisive. And by this gauge many things are evil—such obvious things as theft and murder, and such less obvious things as evil thoughts, pride, and deceit. Here the principle is exactly the same as in the Sermon on the Mount (Matt. 5:21-48), where a harsh word is as sinful as murder and lustful desire as adultery, and where desire for revenge cuts one off from God even more certainly than the more easily recognized sins. Thoughts and desires, motives and emotions—these are the first forms which defilement takes. Mark was more interested in the negative implication, for he adds the note: "Thus he declared all foods clean" (vs. 19). The Jewish food laws are to be rejected. This was what the Roman Christians needed to recognize, for many of their deepest animosities had to do with clean and unclean foods (see the Introduction). But Jesus seems to have been far more concerned with the positive implication. A man defiles himself by what he thinks in his heart. This means that God judges him even by the little careless words he utters (Matt. 12:33-37).

If "understanding" this parable included understanding and obeying all the implications of this revolutionary principle, it is quite clear that the disciples had not understood (vs. 18). It is also quite doubtful if the Church has ever understood. And, to come closer home, which of us has fully understood, if we define understanding by obedience? Yet the teaching remains clear and firm. God knows and judges men according to their hearts (Luke 16:15). As the Good Shepherd he seeks to cleanse them. As a shepherd sent to God's people, Jesus sought to free their hearts from all fears and hatreds. His penetration into God's will for men enabled him to pronounce the pure in heart blessed, and to discern the double-mindedness of those scribes whose heart was far from God (Mark 7:6). It was such duplicity which Jesus recognized as deafness and blindness.

Sheep from Other Folds (7:24-37)

After he had thus defined the source of purity and impurity, Jesus turned away from his home province and went into Gentile country, "the region of Tyre and Sidon." This is the first certain reference in Mark to a ministry beyond the bounds of Jesus' own people. In this Gentile area he traveled quietly and without openly announcing the good news. He understood his vocation in terms of God's redemption of Israel. Nevertheless, contrary to his intention, "he could not be hid." The works which he had done among his kinsmen were now to be paralleled among the Gentiles—exorcism, healings, and feedings. God made him their shepherd also.

Jesus' hesitation to extend his work to Gentiles is strongly accented by the sharp saying about throwing children's bread to dogs. To the Israelites, Gentiles were dogs by comparison to God's Chosen People. The food of Jesus' teaching, which here is clearly identified with power to heal, was primarily intended for that people. The response on the part of this Greek mother was surprising indeed. In her emergency she did not resent the slur, but humbly accepted it. She wanted only a crumb for her daughter. In the face of such lowliness Jesus could not reject her plea.

There is much that is puzzling in this episode. Gentile Christians have always been offended by the harsh tone of Jesus' reference to Gentiles. We cannot recover with certainty his motives. But the main thing is the combination of facts: the demons did not respect lines between one people and another; humility, hope, faith in Jesus as Lord, were from the first demonstrated by Gentiles; the power of God to release men from Satan's clutches was destined to be felt throughout the territory of Satan's control, even though men might not intend it; the Gentile mission had its beginning during Jesus' own ministry. Each of these facts was important for members of the Roman congregations. They naturally saw connections between this trip to Sidonian country and the trip made by Elijah, between this miraculous cure and that wrought by Elijah (I Kings 17:8-24). They also considered this spread of salvation to the Gentiles as a sign of God's reaction to Jewish rejection (Luke 4:25-26).

The next cure (Mark 7:31-37) appears at first sight to add little to previous stories. It certainly proves nothing new about Jesus. Yet we have already seen that the major motive for including
these marvels did not lie in proving the Messiah's power; early
Christians believed in Jesus as Deliverer before these stories had
much attraction for them. About this story we may note that Jesus
was still moving through Gentile lands. This being so, the help offered to a Gentile *man* combined with that given to a Gentile
woman suggests that help is now available to all Gentiles. The exorcism of an unclean spirit is balanced by this case of healing. The
twin stories thus lead to a Gentile hallelujah: "He has done all
things well." Until now the Gentiles (the deaf) had not heard the
good news, now they can; they had not been able to proclaim it
(the dumb), now they do. Therein lies the mystery, for this is a
fulfillment of Isaiah's prophecy that the glory of Lebanon should
be given to God when the ears of the deaf are unstopped and the
tongue of the dumb sings for joy (Isa. 35:1-6). It is by means of
such images that, ever since the Psalms, God's people have sung
his praises.

Two Kinds of Bread (8:1-21)

What binds together these twin healings and the following story
of a feeding? (8:1-10). Probably both took place among Gentiles.
This may be Mark's reason for including two wilderness suppers,
the earlier one being for Jews (6:30-44). We should not forget
that in Rome the Jewish and Gentile Christians had been unable
to eat together at the Lord's Table (Rom. 14). The location "in
the desert" may be a significant link to the prophecy to which we
have referred: "The desert shall rejoice and blossom . . . For waters shall break forth in the wilderness, and streams in the desert
. . . the redeemed shall walk there" (Isa. 35). More significantly,
the work of the shepherd includes, as we have seen, protecting the
flock from enemies (the demons), healing and feeding the sheep,
and, not the least, teaching them the mercy of God. In the familiar Twenty-third Psalm, the spreading of the table is but one of
many ways of describing essentially the same miraculous work of
restoring the soul.

Again, a rather curious feature of the story is a distinction between the disciples and the crowd. Jesus' compassion is directed
to the hungry. He expects the disciples to feed them, however
small their larder. The disciples serve as deacons (Acts 6:1-6).

Only Jesus presides as host—giving thanks (the Greek word from which "Eucharist" comes), breaking the loaves, and giving to the deacons for the congregation. Nothing is said of the disciples' hunger, or of their eating. Their work is exclusively as servants of the sheep. So Jesus feeds his Church miraculously and abundantly. The "seven baskets full" of the broken pieces clearly indicates abundance. The number seven may also suggest the seventy nations of the Gentiles. More interestingly, the "broken pieces left over" indicates that *this* supply of food from God is inexhaustible. (Note "the children's crumbs" of 7:28.) From this table, fragments are available for many others than those being fed at a given setting. This table, with its Host and its food, is intended to include all. Are there four thousand Gentiles present? The fragments indicate that there can be no limit to the number; or, even more strongly, the fragments are a prophecy that countless thousands will be fed from the same supply.

The little company of Lord and deacons seems to be traveling very frequently by boat. They cross the lake (vs. 10) and almost immediately recross it (vs. 13). Why so short a trip? Or, rather, why does Mark give so brief an account of this visit to Jewish territory? Two reasons may be suggested.

1. Mark wanted to stress the contrast between the response among the Jews and the response of the Gentiles. When Jesus had appeared unknown among the Gentiles, a woman had sought him out to fall at his feet in reverence and supplication (7:25). When he touched shore in a Jewish town where he was well known, he ran afoul of the Pharisees with their arguments and their demands for proofs (much like the Jewish Christians of Romans 14). To unbelievers no signs would be given; but to believers he gave freedom from demons, from sickness, and from hunger. What a contrast!

2. The second reason for Mark's brief reference to the encounter with the Pharisees is this: he needed something by way of a background for his next episode, which even with this help remains one of the most difficult bits of dialogue in the Gospel. The dialogue centers on the subject of bread and leaven. Do they or do they not have bread with them? Have they adopted the leaven of the Pharisees? The earlier debate with the Pharisees, leading to Jesus' decision to leave them (like so many Apostles later on), at least suggests that there is something about their leaven which the disciples must shun (vs. 15).

It seems that the Twelve were completely baffled. No less so are modern readers. Yet Jesus had grounds for complaint; they should have understood. What were these grounds? The memory of the baskets of fragments, first twelve and then seven. They remembered, but they did not understand. Mark gives a few clues to the enigma: "blindness" is "deafness" is "hardness of heart" is "misunderstanding." By implication, understanding is equivalent to seeing and hearing and receptivity. Mark thus interpreted in a symbolic way the previous cure of deafness (7:31-37) and the subsequent cure of blindness (8:22-26), and he sets these cures in contrast to the need of the disciples for similar healing.

But now we must ask what can serve as a single object for the seeing-hearing-understanding heart. It has to do with bread, the bread which they have and the fragments in the baskets. Moreover, this bread is set over against the leaven of the Pharisees and of Herod. They are in danger of substituting this leaven for the bread which they have. What is this bread and this leaven?

Here a clue is provided by the seeming contradiction in the text. They have no bread and yet they have one loaf (vss. 14, 16). How can they have one loaf without knowing it? A reference at this point to the Eucharistic language and practice of the Church may help, for regularly the followers of Jesus participated in his body as the broken bread. "The bread which we break, is it not a participation in the body of Christ? Because there is one bread, we who are many are one body, for we all partake of the one bread" (I Cor. 10:16-17). The perennial task of disciples is to discern the body, to see the Lord as one loaf, to feed with faith upon the bread of life. Where the Lord is, there is always one loaf. He is always able to satisfy his hungry flock and to leave ample fragments for others. To trust in him is to see, to hear, to accept, and to obey the good news of God's presence and power. But the danger is always present of eating the other leaven—blindness to the signs of God's Kingdom, proud insistence on proofs, deaf stubbornness in opposing the inclusion of Gentiles, hardhearted reliance upon religious status and political power. If one understands what is bread and what is this leaven, then he will live in a world of abundance; if not, he will live in a world of scarcity, of famine, of rivalry, and of secret despair.

A Blind Man Sees (8:22-26)

In all the previous episodes (the stories of the wilderness sup-

per, the skepticism of the Pharisees, the dilemma of the disciples)
Mark had been speaking of blindness. The account of a cure
comes therefore as a short dramatic climax. Notwithstanding the
baffling character of the Kingdom's presence, men can be helped
to see, as was this man in Bethsaida. There is only one novel element in this account; the cure required two stages—first partial
sight, then clear vision. Having observed Mark's primary concern
with the blindness of the Twelve (vs. 18), we may safely infer
that the two stages symbolize steps in Jesus' cure of them. Probably the first step is represented by the very next episode. In the
previous incident the Twelve had been blind; in the next they gain
partial sight. In either case, both for the Bethsaidan and for the
Twelve, the cures wrought by Jesus were seen by Mark as ful-
fillments of the same prophecy of Isaiah which we have cited.
"The eyes of the blind shall be opened," for God "will come and
save you" (Isa. 35:4-5; 29:17-19).

The Road to Jerusalem (8:27—10:52)

Many commentators on Mark utilize the geographical references to reconstruct a map on which to chart Jesus' movements.
We have not done so in our study of the first half of the Gospel.
Our one exception has been to indicate how Jesus' mission had
first been directed to his home country and only then to the neigh-
boring territories, first to Israel and then to the Gentiles. Apart
from this exception we have concluded that in his references to
various places Mark was more interested in theological than in
cartographical significance. Let us illustrate this by recalling the
role played in his drama by three places: the boat, the wilderness,
the road.

Let the reader recall all that has taken place in the boat. Let us
begin with the scene where Jesus had first enlisted his followers.
They had been in their boats fishing. At his summons they had left
their nets and had followed him, under his pledge to make them
fishers of men (1:16-20). Thereafter no one but his disciples is
pictured as being in the "same boat" with him. In some of the boat
scenes the anonymous crowd was mentioned, but we should notice
in what connections. In a number of scenes, Jesus used the boat
in order to escape the crowd and in order to devote himself to the
needs of the disciples (3:9; 4:35; 5:18; 6:32; 8:10). In one scene,
he teaches the crowd from the boat, quite as if it were his pulpit,

or as if he were casting his net for men (4:1). In three other scenes, he disembarks from the boat in order to struggle with the demons in men and to heal them (5:2, 21; 6:54).

From the first, special significance was attached to joining him in the boat. Why did none but disciples belong there? Because this was the place to share bread with him, the place for him to rebuke their blindness and hardheartedness (6:52; 8:14-21), and the place where he tested their faith by involving them in sudden violent storms. When he had been present but asleep, their fears of wind and sea had quite demoralized them (4:35-41). When he had been absent, they had been wholly unable to make headway against the wind, at least until his amazing arrival (6:45-52). The Christian symbolism in this language is unmistakable.

So, too, in the use of the pictures of the wilderness (or desert, or the country, or a lonely place, for the same Greek noun is translated in these various ways). In the vocabulary of the Early Church, the wilderness was the place where all those lived "who keep the commandments of God and bear testimony to Jesus" (Rev. 12:17). Here was the place as well where the forces of evil were especially active in assailing these followers. This is the place where Jesus had wrestled with Satan (1:12-13), the place of prayer and of vocational renewal (1:35-39), the place of escape from popular clamor (1:45; 6:31), yet the place where God had fed the multitude of pilgrims who, so to speak, had left Egypt and were bound for the Promised Land (6:35; 8:4). This is symbolically the place where those who entered the boat with Jesus were bound to arrive (6:31), yet it is the place where they were expected to feed the shepherdless flock (6:37). One other nuance in this conception must be mentioned: the wilderness is the region where the prophet prepares the road, the highway, of God. Desert-highway; this is a paradox which intentionally expresses the style of living adopted by John, by Jesus, and by his disciples. At the very outset Mark had announced the fulfillment of the prophet's promise: in the wilderness the way of the Lord will be prepared (1:2-3). Thereafter Mark pictures John, Jesus, and all God's children as being at home in the wilderness. All join in preparing God's road. Thus, for example, when Jesus had sent his disciples out on this road (6:8, "journey") to preach repentance like John, he had ruled out any equipment except what was appropriate to this locale.

Mark appeals to this picture of the road sparingly, however, until the second half of his Gospel begins at 8:27. Now the image derives a new dimension, for this teacher is one who knows "the road of God" (see 12:14) and who teaches that road by walking it. Moreover, this road has a very definite terminus, for it is the road to Jerusalem. As in the case of the boat, this image of the road seems to be restricted to Jesus and his followers, because it is the narrow way leading to the Cross. The teaching which Jesus gave on the way drew its meanings from this fact (8:27-38). This is why confusions of the disciples here became especially poignant (9:33-50). Milestones were provided by disclosures of progress toward this terminus (10:17, 32, 46, 52). We should not, of course, infer that all geographical values have been eliminated. Quite the contrary, because in this segment of the narrative Mark makes frequent mention of successive stages. This journey begins in the region of Caesarea Philippi (8:27), then winds through Galilee (9:30), then through Transjordania (10:1), finally to Jericho (10:46) and the suburbs of Jerusalem (11:1). Yes, Mark gives us a very rough itinerary, but even so, he remained aware that this particular road was one which must be walked by every group of disciples in every generation. How this awareness was embodied in his narrative we shall observe as we trace the successive stages of this awesome pilgrimage.

The Coming Confession (8:27—9:1)

From this point on, Jesus concentrates his attention upon those for whom this road will serve as a classroom—his disciples. At the outset, they are confronted with a difficult question—the standing of their teacher. Aware of varying impressions of him, they must form their own. For those who once begin this march, the options among the various answers are limited. Others may think of this Man as a tool of Beelzebul or as insane or as an enemy of the nation. They, however, have seen him as a colleague of John the Baptizer, or as Elijah come again to proclaim the New Age, or as one of the prophets sent to announce God's doom and dawn. All these options, it is clear, were positive evaluations; whichever is adopted, Jesus must be given a hearing as a man sent from God with an important mission to Israel. He continues the work of these authorized messengers. Those who joined in this appraisal would have been constrained to listen and to follow. Yet Peter, speaking for the disciples as a group, tried to say something more: You are the Messiah (vs. 29).

What is the Teacher's response? No word of approval or praise.
No immediate confirmation. Only a command to silence, and the
beginning of the real lesson. Why should they tell no one about
him? Because the simpler titles were adequate? Perhaps. Because
further instruction was needed before they would know what being the Messiah entailed? This is the better answer. It was good
that they should call him "the Christ," but not good enough. They
must know what the title meant, what work the Christ must accomplish, and how he would accomplish it. In all the records
about Jesus, we hear him warning against reliance on verbal confessions alone. Just as he would become what God intended for
him only by obeying God to the end, so they, too, would become
what he intended for them by obeying him to the end. To use the
right title was a good first step. It was like the first step in the re-
turning vision of the blind man (8:24). But apart from another
step, the blind would never see clearly.

Therefore Mark hastens on from Peter's confession to this next
and even more important lesson: "The Son of man must suffer."
This is the lesson the teaching of which would require the re-
mainder of the journey on this road (he "began" to teach). This
lesson was given so plainly that there was no mistaking the meaning. It was because Peter understood the meaning that he protested so loyally and yet so blindly. Loyally? This question must
be answered. To whom was Peter loyal in his protest? To Satan!
Very abruptly Jesus accused Peter of speaking for Satan, of putting Jesus to the test as Satan had earlier tried to do. This Messiah would become the Messiah only in and through his rejection
and death.

This lesson concerning the Messiah's road was welded into the
lesson concerning those who would "come after" him. Each follower must—there is no escape clause—"take up his cross." To
reject the Messiah's road is the same as rejecting the disciple's
road. To believe in him as this Messiah is a lie unless the believer accepts martyrdom for his sake and the gospel's. In short,
his teaching was no easy platitude about the spiritual life. Far
from it. This was an ironclad requirement of actual martyrdom.
Though modern readers can easily dissolve the iron into cobwebs,
Mark's readers could not, for the language reminded them too
harshly of the criminal courts and the prisoner's cell. They knew
that when a Christian was summoned before the judge, he could
"gain the whole world" by denying that he was Christ's follower.

He would be tempted to do so in order to avoid losing or forfeit-
ing his life. In doing so he would be "ashamed" of Jesus and these
very words; he would accept life on terms set by "this adulterous
and sinful generation." But to avoid public disgrace and death in
a Roman court by disowning the Messiah would have only one
consequence: the Messiah would disown his one-time follower in
the final and ultimate court of appeal (vs. 38). Mark and his
readers knew how terrifyingly realistic this language was, for they
had vivid memories not only of the cross on Golgotha but of
many crosses on other hills. Consequently, it was important to
know how far away was this final courtroom of which Jesus had
spoken. Jesus gave the answer: "Truly, I say to you [thus assert-
ing his divine authority], there are some standing here [his eyes
were on his disciples] who will not taste death before they see the
kingdom of God come with power [they will be executed by human hands but not before they have experienced the judging and
redeeming power of God]" (9:1; compare Acts 7:54-56). In
short, Mark believed that just as the Messiah would enter into his
power through dying (vs. 31), so his disciples would see his Kingdom coming with power through their own dying. Losing their
lives for his sake and the gospel's would be the means of salvation
(vs. 35), and this salvation was no farther away than the event
through which they would make their "good confession" (see I
Tim. 6:13). All this was the gist of all the lessons on the road to
Jerusalem (how appropriate this place!), by which the Teacher
explained the meaning of Messiahship to his followers. Their
coming confession of faith, like his, would be given not in a
church but in a courtroom.

The Coming Victory (9:2-13)

God had revealed Jesus' vocation to him in the baptism; he revealed Jesus' vocation to the disciples on the way between Caesarea Philippi and Jerusalem. Peter had confessed Jesus' Messiahship, although only half understanding it. Now God gives his own
testimony. What happened here on the mountain was, of course,
by no means clear to the disciples at the time (vss. 9-10). It was
an augury of the heavenly throne to which Jesus would ascend
after his suffering and glorification. It was a manifestation of the
heavenly glory which God had given to him. In the nature of the
case, a disclosure of such heavenly glory must be described in
terms unusual in human discourse.

The scene was "a high mountain" with its nearness to heaven and its separation from mundane concerns. We recall that Jesus had called and named the twelve Apostles on a mountain (3:13), and that he had himself gone to a mountain to pray (6:46). We will find, too, that in the last climactic week, he will watch Jerusalem from a mountain and disclose to the same three disciples what will be their task after his death (13:3). The mountain, in biblical lore, is the junction point between heavenly and earthly events.

In all early Christian records Peter, James, and John stand as foremost among the Twelve, and as representing the others. Among the first to hear the call (1:16-19), their names headed the list of Apostles (3:16-17). They were present at the first healings (1:29) and were occasionally chosen by Jesus to watch later cures (5:37). All three were later on, though probably before Mark was written, to become martyrs for the sake of the gospel. They, if anyone, had reason to be present on this particular mountain.

The transfiguration of Jesus, accompanied by the white garments of heavenly purity (John 20:12; Matt. 28:3), indicated God's full approval of him. These garments were not only the traditional clothing of angels, but were the garb reserved for all faithful witnesses who were to carry their obedience to the point of death (Rev. 3:4-5; 4:4; 6:11; 7:9, 13). This is a vision of heaven, the invisible reality surrounding earthly actuality. Therefore Moses and Elijah can talk with Jesus. For a moment these three men of God share the same level of existence and can meet face to face. What did they say? Luke answers that they were talking about Jesus' departure ("exodus") which he would accomplish at Jerusalem (Luke 9:31). Mark is content to note the fact of their conversation. What does their presence suggest? That these representatives of the Law (Moses) and the Prophets (Elijah) testify that in Jesus their work is to be completed. That these two previous emissaries of God represent the heavenly world and thereby reveal Jesus' coming translation. That men are correct in associating Jesus' mission with that of Elijah, but are wrong in identifying the two (8:28). That Peter is right in calling Jesus the Christ even though his glory as the Christ awaits his resurrection.

The story invites conjectures of all sorts. If it is a true epiphany, as Mark understood it to be, men using earthly language will be quite unable to capture its full meaning. Mark sees in the story three important points. (1) Peter misconstrues the reason for the

disciples' presence, as if they should build booths on the mountain
for the three men to dwell in. (2) God, speaking from the cloud
of his invisible glory, identifies Jesus as his Son and commands the
disciples to hear him, a command which includes obedience to
such teachings as have just been given (8:34—9:1). (3) Jesus, in
his effort to instruct the disciples, points forward to the Resurrection as if this epiphany were a preview of what would transpire
then. Elijah must come first. In fact, he had already come, and
had been rejected and killed. Jesus had in mind John the Baptist
(Matt. 17:13; 11:14), who had begun the restoration of all
things. Then the Son of Man must carry through his sufferings
and be vindicated against the contempt of men. The reason for
the disciples' presence, a matter vital for the whole episode, was
wholly a matter of anticipation. When they at last should know
"what the rising from the dead meant," they would know that
God had identified Jesus as his beloved Son, greater even than
Moses and Elijah, and that they were under orders to obey him,
even in preference to the Law and the Prophets.

Power to Heal (9:14-32)

The Transfiguration pointed ahead to future things. Therefore
the descent from the mountain marked also a return from that
future prospect to the confusions of the present. The disciples
turned with a jolt from trying to comprehend the coming suffering and heavenly glory of the Son of Man to their everyday tasks.
In these daily concerns they were too submerged in the hubbub to
keep in touch with the glory. They were surrounded by "a great
crowd." They were deeply involved in arguments with the scribes.
They were called upon to heal a man's son by exorcism of a dumb
spirit, and they found themselves quite helpless. The dumb spirit
had more power than they.

When we first read this story, it sounds much like the other accounts of healings, although it gives more complete coverage than
others. Yet it has a different accent which appears as soon as we
note the significant place now held by the disciples. In bringing
the sick boy to the disciples, the father assumed he was bringing
him to Jesus (vss. 17-18). The impotence of the disciples elicited
a penetrating rebuke. They are a "faithless generation" even after
all the time he has spent with them and his endless patience with
them. They will not have much longer to learn the source of his
power (vs. 19).

By contrast with the faithlessness of the disciples, a strong accent falls on the faith of the father. To be sure he is an unbeliever, but he knows it, and has enough belief to call on Jesus for help. It is this halting, hesitant, humble belief which makes help possible (vs. 23). It makes possible even the raising of the dead (vs. 27). The power of Jesus to do this very thing corresponds to the message of the Transfiguration, for Jesus' power to raise the dead is an anticipation of his own resurrection (vss. 9-13). Jesus can do such things because he is now bound for heavenly glory by way of total self-sacrifice.

Chagrined by their impotence and nonplussed by his rebuke, "his disciples asked him privately, 'Why could we not cast it out?'" His answer shows to what an extent this whole story was told for their sakes. After all, they are the men whom he has charged to heal in his name. To their despondent and perhaps petulant query, certain answers had already been given. They were without faith (vs. 19), not able to believe that all things were possible to them (vs. 23). Perhaps they were too concerned with the crowd, or too nettled by the scribes' debates, to give full attention to the demon. Perhaps they did not realize that only by participating in the Messiah's suffering could they participate in his conquest of Satan and his demons. All this may be summarized in one word: prayer (vs. 29)—not as a trick device, or a sure-fire method of gaining results, but as the necessary listening to God in the wilderness where alone Satan's power can be overcome (1:12, 35; 6:46).

That Jesus' concern now lay with his task of training the disciples becomes clear, for he immediately pushed on with them toward Jerusalem. He tried to keep their presence a secret (vs. 30) so that he could spend more time on his teaching. The lesson remained the same (vs. 31)—and their obduracy as well. For Jesus, prayer included accepting the cost of obeying God's will (14:32-42). It was this kind of praying which they did not yet understand.

Proverbs for the Journey (9:33-50)

In this section of the journey we find teaching material almost divorced from narrative settings. No single story, no single situation, unifies the separate proverbs. Each deals with a different topic and has a life of its own. Sometimes what brings them together is merely a common word, which may bear two quite dif-

ferent meanings in adjacent axioms. This fact has led many students to conclude that these axioms first circulated in the Church
as isolated bits of oral tradition. They gravitated together because
of similar verbal links, and because they could be remembered
more easily when thus linked. This sort of explanation can be
checked if one follows the chain backward and notices the links.
"Salt" brings together the three separate maxims of verses 50 and
49. "Fire" connects verse 49 to verse 48. "Fire" in verse 48 is suggested by "hell" in verse 47. The same phrase introduces verses
47, 45, and 43: "If your eye [or foot, or hand] causes you to sin."
Verse 43 is connected to verse 42 by the idea of causing to sin,
although different persons are involved in the two actions. Separate sayings in verses 37-41 all deal with various ways of receiving or welcoming another. Verse 36 follows verse 35 in introduc-
ing a "child" who is an example of one of the "last of all."

When the reader recognizes the fact that this passage presents
him with such a diverse collection of fragments, he will not try to
force them all into a single consecutive discussion. Nor will he be
discouraged if he cannot discern a single thread of meaning.

Mark took pains to provide an introduction to the whole series.
He included the whole series because all deal with duties of the
disciples, which was Jesus' main concern on the way to Jerusalem. But the first axiom was most important to Mark, because it
clinched the meaning for him of the entire road. On this very road
to the Messiah's humiliation, disciples had been quarreling over
places of honor! Nothing could stand in sharper contrast to Jesus'
journey than their private ambitions. In such a setting, therefore,
this axiom received a tremendous thrust: "If any one would be
first, he must be last of all." The explanation of what it meant to
be last of all was provided in part by the phrase "servant of all"
(vs. 35) and in part by Jesus' own rank (vs. 31). One could place
this axiom over the whole of Mark's document as its keynote.

Two of the maxims deal with hospitality granted to a follower
of Christ. If we want to see into what kind of church situation
they fit, we should read Romans, chapters 14 and 15. In Rome
there were house-churches which did not welcome certain Christians, because those strangers were either too careful or too care-
free about observing the scriptural commands (see the Introduction). It is with regard to such a situation that it became unusual
for a congregation to grant table hospitality to a person on no
other ground than that he bore the name of Christ (vs. 41). In

contrast to this inhospitality, the thrust of Jesus' principle was sharp and penetrating: to receive the least attractive and least prominent "child" in the name of Christ was a welcome given to Christ himself, and to welcome Christ was to welcome God (vs. 37; compare Matt. 25:31-45).

A similar situation in the Roman church throws light on the axiom: "He that is not against us is for us" (vs. 40). A man was known to be in town doing mighty works in the name of Christ. "But he," said members of some congregations, "is not truly one of us. We must therefore oppose his work." Such an attitude, in fact, had been taken by various leaders in the Roman churches toward Paul (Phil. 1:15-17). Against this background the Markan proverb insists that no person who truly does a mighty work in Christ's name can be "against us." If he bears this name, we must not add other requirements before accepting him into our fellowship. Thus the proverb is not a plea for expediency in a world where forty per cent are Christians, ten per cent are non-Christians, and the other fifty per cent are neutral. No, the proverb pronounces no blessing on neutrality. Men are either against or for. The real line—and a sharp line indeed in Mark's day—is the line drawn by the name "Christ," and this name is defined by the work of Jesus himself.

True faith is so difficult, and the Messiah so concerned for his "little ones," that every disciple must avoid the risk of causing a brother to stumble (vs. 42; compare Rom. 14:20-21). By the same token a disciple must act ruthlessly toward his own temptations. Entrance into God's Kingdom is so desirable that any sacrifice is justified (vss. 43-47). According to this austere mode of life, in which a single desire of the eye (Matt. 5:28) or a single offense against one's neighbor (Matt. 18:10-14) may spell perdition, "every one will be salted with fire." That is, none of us can avoid God's judgment, with its purging and refining fire (I Peter 1:6-7; 4:12-19). In a different sense, believers are the salt of the earth, so long as they retain their saltiness, that is, their willingness to fulfill the requirements of the Beatitudes (Matt. 5:1-13). In still a different sense, each congregation needs salt (tolerance, mutual sympathy, reconciling attitudes) to preserve and enhance the peace of the Church.

Some of these sayings may be later than the time of Jesus, at least in their present form. Yet all of them reflect the genuine difficulties of faith, whether in Jesus' day or in Mark's. All receive added urgency and clarity from the setting Mark gives to them, for it was in fact Jesus' journey to the Cross which became for his disciples the vivid standard by which their own attitudes and actions were to be salted.

The Good News and the Law (10:1-31)

Chapter 10 opens with a note of advance. The group had moved slowly from the point farthest north (Caesarea Philippi, perhaps near Mount Hermon) through Galilee to Capernaum, on south to Transjordania. When they later come to Jericho (10:46), they will begin the last ascent to the Holy City (11:1, 11). Arriving in Transjordania for the first time (according to Mark's itinerary), they again met the crowds whom Jesus taught and the Pharisees who began testing him. It should be noted, however, that Jesus turned each conversation with non-disciples into efforts to train his disciples. Conversations with the former clarified his attitude toward the Law; conversations with the latter set forth his unique understanding of the Kingdom of God.

First, the Pharisees tested him by asking what the Law dictates concerning divorce. He asked then what Moses had said; they knew the answer and quoted it. Then he told them *why* Moses had allowed a husband to divorce his wife. It was because of their hard hearts. Men whose hearts are far from God, whose minds do not seek God's will, and who rely upon a formal written standard —such men find a written commandment to be necessary. Jesus appealed beyond the Mosaic commands to God's purpose in creating husband and wife (Gen. 1:27). He had made them two in order that they might become one (Mark 10:8). So when they had become one, they were never again to be made two. God's creative act served as the ultimate norm; Moses' command was a compromise with men's self-centeredness and pride.

In his explanation to his disciples the Teacher carried the logic to its true conclusion. Because man cannot change what God has joined, a divorced husband who marries another woman is actually guilty of adultery. The same holds true of a divorced wife if she marries again. According to Jewish law only a husband was permitted to secure a divorce. In Roman law either husband or wife was so permitted. Mark's version covered the latter practice. There is ample evidence that this version was too rigorous for many Christians. Beginning with Matthew's edition, Christians have added various exceptions to the Markan rule (Matt. 5:32).

In doing so, they have misunderstood Jesus' intent. He was not setting forth a new law, which hard hearts could twist to fit their desires. He was simply announcing what God had done in making two one, and therefore what men do in separating two thus joined. Mark knew how difficult this understanding of marriage was, but he let Jesus' teaching for his disciples stand in all its rigor.

The second incident (vss. 13-16) quickly shows that the Kingdom of God is not a matter of keeping laws nor of amassing credit and status. It is a matter of receptivity. One does not need to develop special credits to present as a ticket of admission. Rather he needs to be content with no such credit. Childlikeness had, in Jewish thought, nothing to do with sentimental ideas of innocence or purity. A child had no claims. His status was one of total dependence. He was an example of being least and last. If we are not to hinder children, we are not to hinder anyone—period. If the Kingdom belongs to children, then it belongs to all. To enter, what one needs to do (although this may be the hardest thing) is to be willing to begin again with nothing of one's own (John 3:3; I Cor. 7:29-31; I Peter 2:1-2). Jesus thus tried to teach his disciples both the "impossible" standard of absolute integrity (in the case of marriage) and the "possible" requirement of absolute humility. However difficult it may be, it is possible for anyone to accept the status of a child.

The alternation between teaching non-disciples and teaching disciples is particularly effective in the third incident, which deals still with the so-called requirements for entering the Kingdom. This incident indicates even more clearly both how difficult and how easy it is to become like a child. The line between the eager questioner (vss. 17-22) and the disciples (vss. 23-31) is not very broad. He wants eternal life as do they. Like them he recognizes Jesus as a good teacher and kneels before him in homage. Moreover, he brings his requests when Jesus is setting out again on his road ("journey," vs. 17). We can say that this man comes as near as it is possible to come without taking the same road as a disciple. We should therefore pay close attention to the climax of his story—the one thing he lacked.

He did not lack adequate reverence for Jesus; no, to Jesus his praise was even excessive (vs. 18). He did not lack loyalty to the commandments of God; no, he knew them and had for years obeyed them. He did not lack honesty or sincerity; no, Jesus loved him and did not upbraid him for blindness or hardness of heart.

Then what was the one thing he lacked? He had too many things. His deficiency was his abundance. He had great possessions. Luke (18:18) adds that he was a ruler and Matthew (19:20) that he was young. He could not become a child again, nakedly dependent and defenseless. He could not take the step which would have enabled him to say "having nothing, and yet possessing everything" (II Cor. 6:10). What did he lack? Was it one thing or two? It was one decision in a double form: to give away his wealth and to follow Jesus. To follow Jesus meant total renunciation (Luke 14:25-33). How could a "Good Teacher" whose goodness and whose teaching consisted of being condemned to death (vs. 33) be followed on this very road by a person unwilling to give everything to the poor? Impossible. Following is not following Jesus without selling all other possessions. The one thing this man lacked was decisive.

The Gospel of Mark, however, does not pause to describe what happened to the rich man, but rushes on to focus attention on those who had already embarked on this strange journey. Jesus used the rich man as an object lesson for their sakes. He first underscored the impossibility of such a man's entering the Kingdom. The eye of a needle is too small for a camel. His disciples, although he called them "children" (a status which the other had been unwilling to accept), were astonished at his ruthless logic. "Then who can be saved?" He, in turn, was astonished at their astonishment. Had they not learned that impossible things were possible with God? What was the impossible thing Jesus had in mind? Not that a rich man could follow without becoming poor, but that a rich man could become poor, could become a child. Peter immediately got the point: their own status indicated that God had enabled them to renounce everything to follow Jesus on this road. Whether they had at this time renounced everything becomes a bit dubious when we read the next two paragraphs (vss. 32-45). But Peter's remark, "We have left everything," gives Jesus the opportunity to complete the paradox. The rich man lacked one thing because he held on to what he had. True disciples lack everything but receive one thing. The alternatives were simple, though difficult to understand: either in possessing all things to have nothing, or in having nothing to possess all things. Is this a riddle? If so, the riddle becomes an axiom: "Many that are first will be last, and the last first" (vs. 31). And the illustration of the axiom is provided by the testimony of the Christian community: in surrendering one's family for the sake of the good news (that is, in order to qualify as bearers of this news) they had already "with persecutions" inherited a much larger and more adequate family. How could this be? They were *on the road* (vs. 32), a road which produced simultaneously persecutions and a new family, with eternal life at the end.

Before moving with Mark to the next milestone, we should look back at these previous indications of how this good news was related to the Law (10:1-31). Looking back, we may notice that in all three incidents there is a recurrent interest in the family—the relation of parents to one another (vss. 1-12), of adults to children (vss. 13-16), and of the new family (the Church) to the old (vss. 17-31). All three incidents take place on the same road, all end in instruction to the pilgrims, all presuppose a shift in perspectives produced by faith. Faith in God's creative purpose replaces reliance on the Law and on arguments about interpreting Moses' commands. If by divorce men are quite unable to separate what God has joined together in creation, how much less are they able to cancel the family bonds created by God's miraculous deed in the gospel (compare vss. 10-12 and vss. 27-30). If God has opened his Kingdom only to those who receive it "like a child," how blasphemous are disciples who reject children whose status under the Law is inferior (compare vss. 13-16 and vss. 29-30). If the rich man, though obeying the Law, prizes his possessions above the Kingdom of God, how much more should disciples prize the "hundredfold" possessions granted to them in that Kingdom. In one sense the followers of Jesus must and do become last; in a truer sense, they become first in God's ordering of things (vs. 31); yet this re-evaluation is only realized by those who take the same road—narrow, indeed, but leading to life (Matt. 7:14). This was Mark's message to his Roman readers.

The Coming Baptism (10:32-52)

Mark, however, was under no illusions concerning the difficulty of accepting this message. It was certainly no easier for his Roman brothers than it had been for the Twelve. In fact, the kinship of the two groups was very marked. They were akin in faith and in persecutions (vs. 30). They belonged to the same family with the same destiny. They were both amazed and startled by the same Lord, who always walked ahead of them (vs. 32). They were susceptible to the same kinds of ambition (vs. 37) and, perhaps most decisive of all, they had received the same baptism (vs. 39).

Because baptism was so decisive a step, so characteristic of this new family, Mark was keenly interested in it. To him as to Paul, when a person was baptized, he was united with Christ Jesus (Rom. 6:3, 5). To him as to John, this was nothing less than a new birth from above, like becoming a child again (John 3:3). To him as to both Paul and Peter, baptism required nothing short of being buried with Christ and being raised with him to a new life (Rom. 6:4; I Peter 1:3-7). In baptism a person, once blind, received new sight (John 9:24-38). In three short paragraphs Mark brings together many of these motifs.

In the first of them, he provides a full summary of Jesus' own baptism (vss. 32-34, 38). Here Jesus referred primarily not to the opening scene at the Jordan but to the climactic scene in Jerusalem. The two were not opposed but complementary: the baptism with which the Messiah had been baptized was the baptism with which he would be baptized (vss. 38-39). Predicting this completion of his work, Jesus told the Twelve more fully "what was to happen to him" (vs. 32; see 8:31; 9:12, 31), a full preview of the Passion. What God had ordained for him would be his baptism.

Then Jesus turned to tell his followers about their baptism. The occasion, a very telling one, was the desire for chief places in his glory (vs. 37). Notice the implication of this request. They were now anticipating his triumph and wanted to participate in it. In this respect the disciples had learned something. In the previous days when Jesus had told of coming suffering and vindication, they had not understood (for example, 9:32). Now they comprehend well enough at least to want special seats at his side. Even so, Jesus warns them that they are still profoundly ignorant. Are they able? In this question Jesus gives an epitome of his teaching goal: he wants them to develop this ability. They falsely reply, "We are able," to which he responds with a warning and a promise. The warning is a reminder that the Messiah does not have authority to parcel out privileges. That authority remains vested in God alone. But the promise is something fully within the jurisdiction of the Messiah. Although they are not yet able, they will all in fact participate in his cup and his baptism. In this promise Christian readers detect at once a reference to the two chief sacraments. This is undoubtedly right, but the promise points beyond the sacraments to their consummation in a shared suffering. It is as if Mark were saying to his readers: "Are you baptized? Yes, of course, you are, but this baptism is something which becomes real only when you have carried your own ministry to its end. What that end will be has been disclosed in the story of Jesus."

The ambition of two disciples provoked this promise; the indignation of the other ten provoked the formulation of the new law, the law of the gospel. The disciples in this instance were exemplifying the rule governing Gentile society. Jesus asserts the opposite rule as binding upon his society (vss. 42-43). Here everything is turned bottom side up. Only the slave of all is qualified to govern all. And slavery to others is embodied in the act of dying for them. The only true king, it would seem, is a dead king. It is not at all surprising, then, when we reread the Gospel to find that the rejection of this rule lies behind all the rejections of Jesus, whether by the scribes, the crowds, the rich man, or the disciples. Yet the coming baptism will include the adoption of this rule. The baptism of the disciples will be fulfilled not simply by their suffering and death, but by their becoming slaves of all. This is why the New Testament can speak of all faithful believers as kings (Rev. 1:6, 9; 5:10; I Peter 2:9). When all are kings because all are slaves, such ambitions as those of James and John will be truly senseless.

When he underscored so sharply the blindness to this truth on the part of the Twelve, Mark was not shouting for a crusade against the revered Apostles. He was not holding them especially culpable, because he knew that all disciples share their blindness except when Jesus heals them. The story of the blind beggar serves to suggest the proper response to such teachings. A person must become aware of his blindness and his poverty. He must cry out with the cry of all generations: *Kyrie Eleison* (Lord, have mercy). When Jesus calls, such a one must take heart and rise. He must believe and hope and pray. Then when he receives sight, he will follow Jesus "on the way." To Mark, the true picture of discipleship included both "exposures": the self-centered question of James and John, and the poverty-stricken plea for mercy from the beggar.

The Temple and the Vineyard (11:1—13:37)

Mark's story, as we have seen, was so arranged as to reach its climax in the event of Good Friday. This event had been fore--

shadowed from the earliest preaching of John. It had been more and more clearly anticipated by Jesus ever since he had started from Caesarea Philippi on the journey to Jerusalem. He had sought to prepare his disciples for it, by word and work, and in this preparation he had sought to show them the end of their journey as well as his. As they had pressed closer and closer to this goal, the teaching had become more outspoken (10:33-34). The forecast of coming events was filled with the awesome and the ominous, but with auspicious accents as well, for the salvation of the world would also be accomplished. Both auspicious and ominous counterpoints are to be detected in the music which follows.

Throughout the Passion Story the references to places carry profound overtones. The scene now is Jerusalem, the city of "our father David" (11:10), the place which Jews considered the navel of the earth. Throughout the generations, Israel's hopes had been magnetized by God's promises that all peoples would come to Mount Zion. This spot was dearest of all to God, to Israel, and therefore to the coming Messiah. God had chosen to dwell here; therefore, in loyalty to him, his servants could not forget this city "set on a hill" (see Ps. 137:5-6).

The city's glory was the Temple, where God had chosen to meet his people. Here the faithful brought their burdens of guilt and their caravans of gifts. Here they heard the trumpet sound and lifted up their anthems. Here they awaited news of the promised redemption (Luke 1:5-23; 2:22-52). No true Messiah would ignore this holiest of institutions. It is significant therefore that as soon as Jesus entered the city he "went into the temple" (11:11). Each entrance into city or Temple was the entrance of the true King and Shepherd, for whom the very gates must lift up their heads (Ps. 24:7). Each exit conveyed a sense of the departure of God's glory, a symbol of Israel's rejection of its Lord, or of the Lord's rejection of his people. Each word spoken in the Temple, or each weighty gesture, conveyed its portentous meanings. This Messiah could find no place to abide, either in the city or in the Temple, but must spend his evenings outside the walls in Bethany (11:12), a terrible condemnation in itself. But neither could he stay away from his house if he were to fulfill God's assignment. So the reader of this story must detect the power of his Messiahship by discerning his movements toward the Temple, inside it, and away from it.

Hosannas at the Gate (11:1-10)

The first entrance of the King could not have been a minor or casual event, for he is indeed the King of glory (see Pss. 24, 29, 48, 50). Such an entrance required preparation, and these opening verses indicate how his followers obeyed the Lord's instructions. He would himself furnish everything—the procession, the singers, the mount on which he would ride—all these were provided from outside the city itself. The mount, an untested and unshod colt, must represent the wholly new kind of power which would characterize his reign. The entourage was composed of anonymous and unknown pilgrims. Both the colt and the singers would proclaim the mysterious beatitude, "the meek . . . shall inherit the earth" (Matt. 5:5), and the fulfillment of the prophet's expectation:

Rejoice greatly, O daughter of Zion!

. . . .

Lo, your king comes to you;
    triumphant and victorious is he,
humble and riding on an ass (Zech. 9:9; compare Isa. 62:11).

The arrival of such a king, whose victory would be won by meekness, was an occasion when even the cobblestones would shout in praise (Luke 19:40). For those who had lips to sing, this was indeed the coming of the Messiah in glory. This picture should be set in the same gallery as the pictures of the Messiah's advent in a manger (Luke 2) and of his advent in the new Jerusalem (Rev. 21-22). In it we should hear the hosannas shouted by the humble whenever they welcome the Messiah who came "with healing in his wings" (see Mal. 4:2).

Curses on the Tree (11:11-26)

The story now changes its key from the auspicious to the ominous, for the Savior who comes in the name of the Lord must exercise judgment in that name. We should read this next episode as one intended to show the sharpest contrast to the hallelujahs. We should also read it as a single episode which paints in prophetic black the conflict between the Messiah and his own house (11: 17). A single episode? How can that be? What was the connection between the cleansing of the Temple and the blasting of the tree?

The connection was there, and Mark saw it, because he placed the Temple scene in the middle of the fig tree scene.

A single motif pervades the double scene: the Messiah's judgment on a sinful Israel. The fig tree had produced no fruit for a hungry Messiah; his house had been turned into a cave of brigands. Therefore he whom God had anointed as the Lord of both the tree and the house blasted the one and scourged the other (vss. 14-16). Both acts were signs of his presence in power. He loved Israel and was hated by Israel; therefore his love must be clothed in sternness.

There are difficulties, to be sure, with this interpretation of the text. Why is the fruit tree cursed when it is not the season for figs? (vs. 13). To this conundrum there is no convincing answer. But when we recall how often Israel was spoken of as a tree, how frequently prophets used parables to describe her fruitlessness (for example, Luke 13:6-9), we can perhaps explain this reference to the season as simply a statement of fact. Israel had borne no fruit to give its owner (the same point is made in 12:2-3).

Difficulties appear also in the story of the Temple. Whom did he drive out and why? What did he expect to accomplish? Was he acting as an exorcist of demons, or as a reformer of financial practices? The text invites many diverse interpretations, some of which attack all ecclesiastical institutions and ignore the reality of Christ's love for the Temple (John 2:17). Our reading of the text should do full justice to its prophetic symbolism. For example, the robbery includes not only the frauds practiced by the money-changers against the worshipers but also the stealing of this house from God. Moreover, the thefts from men were not limited to the Temple precincts, as Jeremiah knew, but included the dog-eat-dog practices outside the Temple by men who then took part in the worship (Jer. 7:8-15). In any case, the Messiah's work in the Temple was a prophetic sign of God's wrath, in accordance with God's desire to make his house a place of prayer for all nations. It had been promised that God would bring foreigners and would gather the outcasts to rejoice in the benefits of the Temple (Isa. 56:6-8). It was this promise which Jesus fulfilled and which the priests repudiated, so that this episode becomes an epitome of the Messiah's whole career (John 1:11).

The concluding remarks of Jesus (vss. 22-26) are even more of a riddle. Do they belong here or elsewhere? Perhaps these proverbs concerning faith, prayer, and forgiveness should be separated completely from this context. Yet Mark thought that they belonged here, and if we are correct in our understanding of the symbolism, they do belong. If the fig tree signifies Israel's fruitlessness, then it also signifies that earthly power which seemed most insuperable to Jesus' followers and the greatest source of their despair. If we had asked Mark's readers what, in their judgment, was the greatest single obstacle to the triumph of the gospel, many of them would have answered: the implacable hostility of the leaders of the Roman synagogues. Considering this hostility, what was the likelihood that the mission of the Church could succeed? To them "faith in God" meant confidence that "this mountain" (the total weight of Israel's resistance) would be "cast into the sea." For them to pray was to ask God for the triumph of his gospel over this enmity. Could such a prayer be answered? Jesus' word (supported by his action) assured the readers that this prayer would be answered, provided it voiced not their vengeance but their forgiveness. They must forgive as he had forgiven (Luke 23:34). They must have as deep a desire for Israel's salvation as he had demonstrated. When we view the whole episode in this fashion, it conveys much the same message as Paul's letter to the same church (Rom. 9-11). Moreover, it was a preview of Jesus' own struggle in Gethsemane and on Calvary, where his faith was set in monumental opposition to the massive sins of the world, and where by prayer and forgiveness he received the victory for which he prayed (14:32-42; 15:16-39).

A Parable Against the Tenants (11:27—12:12)

Israel had been called by God to be a light to the nations. The Holy City had been designed to be a magnet to draw the tribes of men. The Temple had been established as God's dwelling and therefore the sanctuary for all peoples (11:17). The priests, scribes, and elders (vs. 27) had been appointed to welcome foreigners and outcasts in the name of the Lord (Isa. 56:6-8). The Messiah had been sent to bring to realization all these things. But was he the Messiah? That was the key to everything else. The guardians of Israel were duty-bound to raise the question, "Who gave you this authority . . . ?" (vs. 28). Why did Jesus not give a direct answer? We do not know. Perhaps it was because recognition of his authority must come from God and therefore from the heart. As usual he turned the burden of proof upon the questioners. What about John? Or rather, what about his baptism? Obviously Jesus knew that the authority for this baptism was from heaven (9:13). But did the Temple leaders know it? They pled agnostic neutrality (vs. 33). Actually they had denied God's initiative in John's work of preparing a highway in the desert (1:2-3).

It is an interesting lesson in the varieties of language to examine the subsequent story as a precisely parallel teaching (though in vastly different idiom). The paragraph we have just read is a pronouncement story, a narrative whose purpose is to give a trenchant pronouncement. The next paragraph is a parable, an imaginative story about something that happened once upon a time. Yet Jesus addressed the same company, and the thrust of his message was much the same. For they had rejected his authority and in rejecting him had rejected the God who sent him. Actually in its form the story is closer to allegory than to parable, for almost every detail has an algebraic equivalent. The people of God are now represented by the vineyard, a usage quite common in Scripture. God is the man who had planted this vineyard (12:1) and had given it all it needed to produce a harvest. The tenants are those stewards to whom God had entrusted the vineyard's care and who had accepted the task of producing the harvest—in other words, the leaders of Israel. But the benefits had not come to God; they had been embezzled by his appointed leaders. They no longer recognized the owner of Israel, nor did they concede that Israel belonged to him. When God sent messengers (his servants the prophets) to collect his share of the harvest, the tenants had skeptically asked, "By what authority . . . ?" (11:28). With the sending at last of the Son, they argued that with him out of the way there would be no further challenge to their position. They would become in fact the sole owners. So they killed him (Jesus, of course) and cast him out of the vineyard (of this, the Crucifixion outside the city wall was a symbol). This is the story of the vineyard, but it parallels the debate with the priests (11:27-33), the cleansing of the Temple, and the blasting of the fig tree. In fact, it is a sharply etched summary of the story of Jesus, yes, even of the story of Israel from beginning to end.

"What will the owner of the vineyard do?" He will not touch the vineyard itself. His people are holy. Has God rejected them? No (Rom. 11:1). The love of God for them will force him to save them from their leaders. One set of tenants will be destroyed,

in spite of the obvious fact that they had succeeded in their declaration of independence. Had they not killed the Son? Yes, but
his death will be reversed by his resurrection. Or, in the language
of the Psalm, which substitutes the picture of a temple for that of
a vineyard, God will choose as the cornerstone a block of stone
which the masons had thrown away (Ps. 118:22-23; I Peter 2:7).
Every story in this section thus became for Christian readers a
tiny etching of the longer Passion Story which would follow.

Traps Set for the Son (12:13—13:2)

According to the allegory the farmers simply killed the son
whom the owner had sent. But that is a figurative summary of the
whole story. Actually, this murder took place over several months,
if not years, and had its source in their deafness to his message.
Mark, however, detects a trap in every altercation over Jesus'
teaching, a trap set for the purpose of destroying him, a trap which
in fact succeeded, in that they accomplished his death, and yet
failed, in that he used each trap as an opportunity to teach God's
will. The scribes used three traps (12:13-34); in rebuttal their
quarry launched several attacks upon them (12:35-44). At least
this was the order in which Mark arranged this last debate between Jesus and the "tenants."

The first trap was dexterously laid. The Herodians as supporters of the Roman puppet were eager to get evidence of treason
against Caesar. The Pharisees as spokesmen for God and his Law
wanted to alienate Jesus from loyal Jews who rejected the sover-
eignty of the emperor. If Jesus said, "Pay the taxes," he would be
a traitor to Israel; if he said, "Do not pay," he would commit
treason against Rome. Either answer would destroy him. Jesus,
however, proved even more adept at setting traps. "Bring me a
coin," he said. He put them on the defensive, for they were Jews
who carried money on which the image of Caesar was inscribed.
They were self-confessed idolaters. Moreover, the image proved
that this money was coined by the emperor and therefore belonged to him. They had answered their own question, and were
caught in their own trap. But this was more than a matter of
adroit dodging. With his final command, "Render to Caesar . . .
and to God," Jesus forced them to decide for themselves which
things belong to one king or to the other. This is in truth the demand of God, compelling man to determine for himself the proper
ownership of everything, down to each penny. In the preceding

parable Jesus had made clear how this decision had already been made by his antagonists (12:1-12). What belongs to God? Jesus gave his own verdict by giving his life. It proved quite impossible to trap such a man, and equally impossible to avoid his trap.

The Sadducees set a different kind of trap, one which dealt with speculation concerning life after death. They had often challenged the scribes with this riddle, because the Sadducees denied the existence of such life while the Pharisees defended it. Both appealed to the Pentateuch as final authority. If there is an existence after death—an unlikely possibility, according to the Sadducees —what will be the situation for a woman who had, in accordance with Mosaic prescriptions (Deut. 25:5), become in turn the wife of seven husbands, and the widow of all seven? "Whose wife will she be?" The Pharisees had never been quite able to meet this dilemma, for obvious reasons.

Jesus' answer is still not intelligible to those who base their arguments and conjectures on the same grounds. These grounds, he insisted, reflect ignorance both of the Scriptures and of God's power (vs. 24). Faith in life after death emerges out of a direct knowledge of God's power rather than out of human egoism. Resurrection is not to be confused with reanimation, nor is life in heaven to be confused with life on earth. Resurrection means transformation. The Apostle Paul later gave perhaps the most adequate clues to the radical changes which are wrought in that transformation (I Cor. 15:35-57). Death will involve the change from one glory to another, from one body to another, each given according to God's purpose. When men become "like angels in heaven" (vs. 25), their whole being will be transfigured (9:2-3; Rev. 7:9-17). The cleverness of the Sadducees ignored God's power to accomplish such things. Worse than this, they denied that God himself is alive, that is, that he is the very ground of life. Because he lives, Abraham, Isaac, and Jacob also live. In his livingness and theirs, men may find the starting point for their thinking. Where God lives, there live also all who belong to him. Faith in the resurrection rests on personal knowledge of this life and this power. The passing of time, therefore, does not increase the distance from the dead patriarchs; rather they are alive in the present. Their resurrection is reality; men should begin to reason about such matters by recognizing that reality.

One of the scribes, a Pharisaic opponent of the Sadducees, approved this answer (vs. 28). He therefore posed a question on which many rabbis had been deliberating. What is the best summary of all the laws? When we list all of the divine commandments, which should be placed at the head of the list, as including all the others? Jesus did not evade this question, because it was entirely legitimate. His answer was explicit and direct. Moreover, this scribe approved Jesus' ruling, and Jesus approved his approval (vs. 34). In the midst of debates, even in the shadow of bitter conflict, there emerged this point of agreement between the Son and the tenants of the vineyard. Mark did not want the Roman disciples, embroiled in the same conflict, to forget that Church and synagogue belonged to the same Israel. They were addressed by the same God, and they affirmed loyalty to his commandments. Only in one respect did Jesus qualify his approval: "not far from the kingdom." How far was this? As far as the rich man in 10:22? As far as the scribes of 12:38-40? Or as near as the widow in 12:44? Or as far as the verbal recognition of the first law is from its embodiment in love? With Jesus' example before him, Mark seems to be saying to his readers in Rome: "You should not be too eager to deny that your enemies may love God. At any moment you may meet a scribe like this, ready to be instructed in the Kingdom" (Matt. 13:52; Acts 23:9). This message is in fact the same as that taught a little later by Joseph of Arimathea (15:43).

Mark says nothing more about this scribe; he quickly turns to another item of debate with the scribes. They recognized that the Messiah was to be the Son of David, for the Scriptures had taught it very plainly (Ps. 18:49-50; Amos 9:11-12; Isa. 9:2-7). But Jesus appealed to David himself as the traditional author of the Psalms. David had been guided by the Holy Spirit, who inspired the prophets, to call the Messiah not only "son," but much more significantly "Lord." This became a favorite text among the Christians, for it indicated many things about their Master: his succession to David's place, his power over his enemies, his priesthood, his throne on Mount Zion (Ps. 110; see also Matt. 22:44; Luke 20:42-43; Acts 2:34; Heb. 1:13; 5:6). Now in the very city of David, when the prophecy was fulfilled, the scribes could not discern his hidden authority as David's Lord. Reliance on the Scripture had aggravated their blindness.

On a number of occasions in earlier chapters Jesus had cautioned his disciples against the leaven of the scribes (8:15). Now again he has his students in mind. What made such a warning necessary? If we itemize the faults of these men, only one is obviously wrong: the devouring of the houses of helpless widows, and even this meal was fully enjoyed within the Law and without conscious cruelty. The other faults are far less terrible. One seems a perfectly laudable desire—to deserve the dignified long robes of respected leadership, the ceremonious greetings of the less noble citizenry, the seats set aside in the churches for prominent members, the places of honor at banquets. Is there any society which does not grant these recognitions, or which does not encourage the desire for them? "Long prayers" seem to be the rule in every religious company. Who is there who, if he prays at all, is guiltless? And who is free of the element of pretense? Yes, if these things are terrible, then Jesus was wise in warning his disciples. In mentioning the scribes, he chose not the worst but the best individuals in the life of Israel, and looking squarely at his followers said, "Beware." In this case as in others, Jesus measured uncleanness not by external righteousness but by the wishes and words which spring from the heart (7:14-23).

He measured money with the same scales. He noticed that the rich men subscribed large sums to the Temple budget. Was this wealth the profit from foreclosed mortgages on widows' homes? What did it say about their hearts? And he noticed the widow who quietly and almost secretly put in her last coin. Was she the one who had been robbed? Even that is unimportant to Jesus. For he measured the gift by the giver's heart. By those scales, the penny was a larger sum than the rest of the budget. Is this poetic exaggeration? Or is it God's disclosure of what money means to him?

Having deflated the value of the currency, Jesus turned to the deflation of the most sacred building itself. In a sense this is the climax of his debates with the scribes and priests. His authority exceeded that of the vineyard owner of 12:9. He knew the power of God and therefore the truth of the resurrection (12:24-27). He was the Lord; in serving him every scribe must seek the last place rather than the first (10:35-45; 12:35-39). He was a widow's son, whose poverty cheapened all the gifts of rich men. But what now about his evaluation of the Temple itself?

We have mentioned the Temple's sacredness and its holiness. We recall how old it was—more than nine centuries. We should recall how gigantic and impressive it was, with huge stone buildings, set in an immense square courtyard, surrounded by thick walls, on the summit of the hill. Nothing in the landscape of Jesus' day could match it for splendor, for strength, for permanence.

All this must have been in their eyes when the disciples said, "Look, Teacher." But there was something else, too. This Temple with its vast resources was their enemy. It would soon be instrumental in killing the Messiah and his Apostles. It would continue to be the stronghold of resistance to the Church. Within its courts the word of the chief priests was law, at least so long as the Roman governor did not countermand it. Who, then, can fight against such massive power, such agelong prestige, such holiness? (compare Rev. 13:1-10). Yet this very Man, this layman among the professional churchmen, this poor man whose only power was that of meekness, chose to fight against it. He uttered a curse much more explicit than the blasting of the fig tree, much less enigmatic than the story of the vineyard: "There will not be left here one stone upon another." It was this prophetic woe which would soon play an important role in his trial and condemnation (14:58; 15:29; John 2:19).

A Warning from the Fig Tree (13:3-37)

The careless reader may well overlook the strategic location of this next body of teachings. Jesus sat (the usual posture of the Jewish teacher) on the Mount of Olives (recall the symbolism of the mountain). He sat "opposite the temple," looking down at it and across the steep ravine cut by the Kidron. The Temple, as we have just noticed, was the most ominous and powerful obstacle to his ministry. This was instruction intended only for his intimate friends, that is, for those to whom he had promised his cup and his baptism (10:39), those who would experience the implacable hatred of the world. Moreover, the timing was also strategic. It was immediately before the Passover and therefore the last long opportunity Jesus had for lecturing this class before the hurrying momentum of events prevented such lecturing. Yet those coming events were very much in view. (The second-mile student should try to discover all the cross references between chapter 13 and subsequent chapters; for example, the "watch" of 13:37 and 14:38; the darkened sun of 13:24 and 15:33.) Although the Cross of Jesus loomed ahead, these teachings were more concerned with preparing the Apostles for their own crosses. They were the servants to be put in charge of his house by "a man going on a journey" (13:34). What will they do during his absence? How will they then meet the sudden squalls on the sea? (4:35-41). Against what dangers must he forewarn them? Notice again the two times which Mark had in mind. There is the time of the Church's suffering from arrests instigated by synagogues, governors, and kings (13:9). Their faithfulness during that time would depend on their memories of what Jesus had taught during the time of his suffering from the same opponents. This need explains the imperious tone of these teachings and Mark's sense of their importance.

The teachings appear to be prompted by the disciples' nervous query, "When will this be . . . ?" The antecedent of the pronoun "this" is uncertain. The casual reader will suppose it refers to the crumbling of the Temple buildings. Not so. The following question is much more inclusive in its reference to "these things." The question deals with the consummation of the warfare between Jesus and all his enemies, human and demonic. It was clear that this warfare produced an unparalleled reversal in all things, in permanence and power, wealth and greatness, sin and righteousness. But what would be the sign that this warfare was about to be ended? The question has bothered Christians ever since. Perhaps we start aright by observing that Jesus, as so frequently is the case, did not really answer the question, but took their asking as an opportunity to warn them against both false hopes and false fears.

It was a false hope to follow those who would come in the name of Christ, saying, "I am he!" They must avoid such feverish excitement (vs. 6). It was a false fear to judge from international conflict that the end was at hand. They must not give in to such alarms (vss. 7-8). The end would not come as soon as that, or with that kind of harbinger.

Fear, of course, would not be a sin, but certain fears would be. They should not be afraid of their enemies, but be concerned only with how to give their testimony fearlessly (vs. 9). God had a purpose in allowing them to face tribunals and terrorism (vs. 10): the gospel must thus be preached in weakness to powerful men of all nations as Jesus preached from the cross to the centurion (15:39). They were not to worry in advance over these courtroom scenes. The Holy Spirit could be counted upon to speak through them (as he spoke through Jesus to Caiaphas and Pilate). Concern for dating the end must be replaced by concern for enduring to the end (vs. 13). For both this hatred and this endurance, Jesus' own story provided the best illustration.

Nothing could make clearer the absolute antithesis between a world order in which "you will be hated by all for my name's sake" and a kingdom in which the God of love redeems all for his own sake. So absolute was this contradiction between hatred and love that the imagination staggers at the effort to conceive it, or to say how the transition could take place from one world to the other. Jewish seers had long adopted the most extreme language to indicate what would happen in that Day. Mark employs their visions here in verses 14-18. The upshot of these verses was simply to stress the truth that before God's love could be made the basis of world order there would necessarily be "such tribulation as has not been from the beginning of the creation" (vs. 19).

Yet the sequel which we expect to find is simply not there. These verses do not describe the accomplishment of all things (vs. 4). Even after inconceivably terrible tribulation, the end does not come. Even after such dread signs, the disciples must not be trapped by them into following false messiahs and false prophets. They are forbidden to base their own hopes or fears upon external crises of this sort. Their Messiah has come. Their primary duty is endurance in his name. Nothing will be done to make their baptism any easier than his.

This does not mean that there would be no triumph of the Kingdom of love over the realm of hatred. Men would see the Son of Man enthroned with majestic glory and terrible power, coming to rule over men and to gather his people, the living and the dead (vss. 26-27). This is exactly the same message which Jesus gave the high priest (14:62), and it is implied in his declaration concerning the Temple's destruction (13:2). The time will come, because it has come, when "the kingdom of the world has become the kingdom of our Lord and of his Christ, and he shall reign for ever and ever" (Rev. 11:15). But they will not see him until simultaneously the usual light for seeing has failed (13:24) and until the powers which rule men have been dethroned (13:25).

Such are the signs which disciples may well notice, tokens that the usual standards of power and glory have been shaken by the power and glory of the Risen Lord. When this kind of earthquake shakes their world, then they will know that he is very near, "at the very gates." Otherwise his work, his mission, his salvation, would decay and pass away, while the world order that had been challenged by his work would remain forever unchanged. So, to put the message of this paragraph (vss. 28-31) in a word, Jesus made despair impossible for his followers. Are they tempted to despair because summer is so far away? Yes, but if they believe in his glory and his power, they will see the fig tree's leaves (vs. 28). Are they tempted to despair because of the unbroken chain of generations one after another? Yes, but they must remember that his promise is to their own generation (vs. 30). Do heaven and earth appear unchanged by his mission and commission? Yes, but his words are more eternal even than they. Is such despair inevitable and such faith impossible? When a disciple thinks so, he should recall such words as these: "all things are possible with God" (10:27). For Mark, at least, Jesus had defined faith by an impossibility which had become possible: God's redemption of the world through a crucified Messiah.

That was why Mark chose a particular parable to conclude this concluding lecture by the Messiah. Here is a final warning against sign-watching and time-charting. Not even the Son knows the day in advance (vs. 32). The test of a disciple's faithfulness is not the accuracy of his predictions but his patience and endurance in watching. But the man who sits at the door scanning the horizon is not watching. No, true watching is accomplished when each servant performs his assigned work (vs. 34). To sleep is to forget that this work has been assigned by the Lord, and to delay its completion. To watch is not anxiety over heavenly cataclysms but obedience to the very Person who has assigned the task. The nature of this Person and his assignment are both described perfectly in the Passion Story. Suddenly, this crucified Lord will come to those whom he has hired. Will they be alert and ready? Only if they watch as he watched in Gethsemane. This was the final command of Jesus to all disciples in every century, the warning of the fig tree: "What I say to you I say to all: Watch" (vs. 37).

The End of the Beginning (14:1—16:8)

We have followed Mark in calling the whole story "the beginning of the gospel" (1:1). This final act, therefore, may properly be called the end of the beginning. In this act the various episodes are tightly woven together into a single, swiftly moving chain. The struggle steadily becomes more intense, each word and deed becomes more heavily weighted with meaning, each verse becomes a solemn summary of all that has happened earlier as well as a pregnant forecast of what will happen thereafter. At every step historians discern riddles and are far from agreement on how to solve them. Yet even more tremendous dilemmas are posed for the believer, inasmuch as the story is told as a preview of what following on this "road" will entail for him. Our present study will stress these dilemmas, because Mark was intent upon the story's impact on his Roman brothers, and we, too, are addressing our comments to believers.

Three Forecasts (14:1-16)

Mark introduced the Passion Story by weaving together three different types of preparations. The first was accomplished in Jerusalem by the priests and scribes, whose plot, hatched in the Temple whose demolition Jesus had announced (13:2), required the help of a disciple. The second was accomplished outside the Holy City in Bethany, not in the homes of "the clean," but in the home of a leper, where Jesus ate supper with his disciples (14:3-9). The third was accomplished in the deliberate movement by Jesus from Bethany into Jerusalem to celebrate the Passover (vss. 12-16). Mark detected the symbolic weight of these three places.

Mark also took care to accent the times. All three forms of preparation pointed straight toward the Passover. The ominous preparation by the enemies took place two days earlier (vs. 1). Preparation by the leper and the woman of Bethany took place one day earlier (vs. 3). On that same day, Jesus made arrangements through his disciples for the Passover meal (vss. 12-16). If we are to follow this schedule, we need to remember that the Jews reckoned days from one sunset to the next. Supper marked the beginning of a day. The first day of Unleavened Bread introduced an eight-day memorial of deliverance from Egypt. This first day began with supper and ended in the afternoon, "when they sacrificed the passover lamb" (vs. 12). Passover itself was a single day, introduced by the evening meal (vs. 17), the second of the eight days of Unleavened Bread. According to Mark's calendar, this particular Passover fell on the day before the Sabbath (Saturday). The Crucifixion took place on the Passover Day, and on the same day the burial (15:42). Nothing happened on the Sabbath, but the story began again (16:1-2) on the first day of the week (Sunday).

All three forecasts, then, point toward the Passover Day, the day of Jesus' death. The first forecast was drawn up by those who sought that death as a means of defending the Temple, the Law, and themselves. These were the men of whose "leaven" the disciples had been warned, whose leaven Judas ate on the day of Unleavened Bread (14:10-11). With him they struck a bargain (a truly demonic covenant), the conclusion of which was reached on the next day, the Passover itself.

Between telling how the plot had been arranged (vss. 1-2) and how Judas had shared in it (vss. 10-11), Mark told of an important supper in Bethany (vss. 3-9). The host was a leper; the guests, Jesus and the Twelve, including Judas. It established, as did all meals in Israel, a covenant between the host and his guests, for each meal bound the people together in a pact of mutuality. In this case all would have been infected, or, as Mark saw it, all made clean. During the meal an unnamed woman gave a prophecy by anointing Jesus with a very expensive perfume. Some were angry at the waste and "reproached her." But breaking into their protests and her silence, Jesus revealed the beauty of her gift. She had anointed his body for burial, although this was usually done after death (16:1); she had prophesied that in the coming days the disciples would be left alone (vs. 7); and she had established a permanent memorial in the later preaching of the gospel, which would everywhere proclaim salvation by this death (vs. 9). The beautiful action of the woman had thus provided a sharply etched contrast to the actions of the chief priests and the traitorous disciple.

Having narrated what preparations had been made by these enemies and by this woman, Mark then gave the account of Jesus' own preparations. His commission, as at earlier strategic moments, had fallen upon two disciples (11:1; 6:7). He had sent them as scouts into hostile territory, like the spies sent out by an earlier Jesus (Joshua 2). He knew that they would find even in the stronghold of his foes a householder who would welcome them and provide a room for their meeting—similar, perhaps, to accommodations in some of the house-churches of Rome (see Introduction) and to the welcome accorded to itinerant Apostles (6:10). In the houses of Palestine, the upper room, often on the roof, would be the place for receiving guests. This room would be large enough. Here disciples would prepare the meal, but they must do it at the Master's command, and at a place of his selection, for he would be their host at this table. Thus Mark prepared the reader for the story to follow. He gave these pictures, separate yet interlocking, of the different initiatives which had been taken by the enemies, by the serving woman, and by the serving Teacher.

The Covenant in Blood (14:17-31)

It is easy to overlook the fact that all that transpired from this evening (vs. 17) until the burial (15:46-47) took place during a single day, beginning with the supper and ending with the shutting of the tomb. Therefore it is entirely natural that the conversation at supper, since it was the final rendezvous of this group, should deal with the meaning of all that would happen on that day. Each word requires for its understanding the entire story; moreover, both to Jesus and to Mark, the story embraced both what men accomplished and what God accomplished in these events.

The terrible, redemptive day began with supper. But how did the supper begin? With the awful announcement, "One of you will betray me" (vs. 18). And how did the supper end? With the equally paralyzing declaration, "You will all fall away" (vs. 27). The account of the supper itself proceeded within these two brackets, these two announcements which would come true within a matter of hours. These brackets indicated how completely Jesus was concerned with his disciples. It was for their sakes that he broke this bread, and for their sakes, also, that Mark told the story. The story clearly indicated where Mark intended to place the accents. Notice how the infamy of the betrayer was stressed: "one who is eating with me . . . one of the twelve, one who is dipping bread in the same dish with me." And how the denial was described: "the sheep will be scattered . . . you will deny me three times . . . 'I will not deny you' . . . they all said the same." There was a contrast between betrayal and denial: one would betray but all would deny. Each of the Twelve asked if he were the traitor, but all denied their denial, stoutly affirming their readiness to die with him. Yet Jesus knew their hearts; his prophecy would come true.

We must not overlook, however, one feature in the story. Between the brackets, in full awareness of their fears and self-deceptions, Jesus broke the bread and poured out the cup for them and for many others. Thereafter none could deny that it was "while we were yet sinners Christ died for us" (Rom. 5:8). None could trust his hold on Christ, but all could trust Christ's hold on them. Knowing this, they could preserve his testimony to their treason; the same testimony assured them of his love, for their Master, in eating with them, had prophesied more than their denials. He had prophesied the saving value of his death, promised them to sup with them again in God's Kingdom (see Matt. 26:29), assured them of his meeting them in Galilee, where he would again gather the scattered sheep. In the preceding lecture on the Mount of Olives he had taught them that their primary concern must be to endure to the end (13:9-13); now his actions spoke louder than his words. This was how he had endured to the end, and how in doing so he had accomplished their redemption, for at his orders they all drank the "blood of the covenant" (vs. 24).

We must say something about the meaning of Passover and Unleavened Bread to first-century Jews and Christians. To both groups this was the most sacred season of the year, because it celebrated anew the deliverance of Israel from Egyptian bondage and anticipated anew the fulfillment of all God's promises. The hymns praised God for his rescues. The Scripture enabled each father to instruct his son in the holy tradition (Exod. 11-14), telling how all the hosts of the enemy had been defeated and the Covenant people had escaped from slavery to Pharaoh. Eating this meal alerted the people for a hasty pilgrimage, on which they would again forsake all their possessions and set out toward the Promised Land. "In this manner you shall eat it: your loins girded, your sandals on your feet, and your staff in your hand; and you shall eat it in haste" (Exod. 12:11). It was a time for ridding every house of the old leaven (I Cor. 5:6-8), for holy assembly and grateful songs. All these meanings carried over into Christian observance of the Eucharist, for the New Covenant in Jesus' blood continued and fulfilled the Covenant which God had sealed in the sacrifice of the paschal lambs (Exod. 12:13). Perhaps a part of the hymn sung by Jesus and his disciples was Psalm 114:

> When Israel went forth from Egypt,
>   the house of Jacob from a people of strange language,
> Judah became his sanctuary,
>   Israel his dominion.

The Night Watch (14:32-52)

The journey to the Mount of Olives was no casual sequel to the supper but its continuation, for the meal and the lonely watching, linked together by the Hallel Psalm, were intrinsic parts of the same celebration. Especially was this true for Christians who

thought of their own life as that of pilgrims on a new Exodus.
They recalled, therefore, with added understanding, God's command concerning the night following the meal:

> It was a night of watching by the LORD, to bring them out of
> the land of Egypt; so this same night is a night of watching
> kept to the LORD by all the people of Israel throughout their
> generations (Exod. 12:42).

Of what did such watching consist? Jesus gave a complete demonstration. It consisted of prayer in solitude, without support from
anyone else (vs. 32). Of agony of spirit, as distressing as the
pangs of death (vs. 34). Of accepting the hour and drinking the
cup, the cup which contained the Covenant blood (vss. 24, 36).
Of resisting the temptation to place his own will above the
Father's (vs. 36). Of accepting, without resentment, or fear,
betrayal by a follower "into the hands of sinners" (vs. 41).

This "night of watching by the LORD" demonstrated also what
was meant by sleeping. Point by point, the story embodied the
point of the parable in 13:32-37. The Lord commanded his servants to watch, and then left them alone. Three times he came to
them during the night to find them asleep. They did not understand or share his praying, his suffering, his struggle with God's
will, his sorrow over the hatred of the world. They had not
prayed, but had in fact succumbed to Satan's testing of their flesh
(vs. 38). They did not quite know why Jesus reproached them,
what was transpiring in his struggle, or why they should not
snatch some rest. Whereas Judas had betrayed him by action, they
betrayed him by complacency and insensitiveness. This was the
way the story spelled out the simple word "asleep."

During their sleep he was betrayed by one of them. The kiss of
Judas stamped Judas as more guilty than the crowd armed with
clubs. In kissing Jesus, Judas identified him so that strangers
could arrest the right person, but the kiss revealed more about
Judas than about Jesus.

The events bore out Jesus' prophecy, not only that one would
betray him but also that all would deny him. When the test came,
"they all forsook him." Even the slight exceptions proved the rule.
One used his sword in a halfhearted way, but such an action was
ill-advised and futile (vs. 47). Another started to follow (vs. 51),
but not for long; when the soldiers seized him, he panicked. His
momentary allegiance, symbolized perhaps by the loose linen robe

(compare with Rev. 3:4, 5, 18), turned to flight, and he left with the soldiers the token of his discipleship, his very nakedness signifying his shame (compare with Rev. 3:17; 16:15). No, the arrest showed how Jesus had long been ready for it, and how all the others were ill-prepared, whether they relied on "swords and clubs" (vs. 48) or on scuttling away into the darkness. Gethsemane itself had been a courtroom with its own verdicts of innocent and guilty.

The Twin Trials (14:53-72)

Now the scene shifted, and the same persons faced a trial in which the secrets of their hearts would be revealed in more official actions. The story continued to deal simultaneously with the trial of Jesus and the trial of the disciples, in the person of Peter. For the sake of clarity we should separate these two trials and examine each in turn.

Before whom was Jesus tried? All the recognized leaders of Israel, from the scribes and elders through the priests to the high priest. In them was vested the right to represent and to govern Israel. It was the "whole council," the Sanhedrin, which now heard the formal examination of witnesses. We would misread the story if from the outset we labeled this court too blackly as totally corrupt. Notice that Jesus nowhere castigates their personal integrity and nowhere repudiates the legality of the proceedings. The pathos of the situation was all the greater because they were the legitimate and reputable rulers of God's people. To them he had been sent as the long-awaited deliverer. For them he had done his assigned task. To be condemned by them was harder to accept than death itself. For Israel to deliver its Messiah to the Romans for execution would be a stupendous sign of the failure of his hopes and his mission.

Of their desire to convict him, the story leaves no doubt. Yet the first stage of the trial frustrated this desire. The testimony was quite inadequate to justify the charges (vs. 55). To be sure, witnesses presented evidence that was damning enough, but no two of them would agree. When Jesus was invited to answer his accusers, he preserved strict silence. He would not debate the case with them. When no conclusive evidence could be marshaled to secure a conviction, the high priest became desperate. He asked Jesus point-blank: "Are you the Christ, the Son of the Blessed?" (vs. 61). This was the pivotal moment in the trial. Would he confess or not? We do not know what answer the high priest expected to get. Nor does the reader at this point know what to expect. We cannot with assurance recover why Jesus at last answered so directly and unequivocally. Was it because Israel, through its supreme representative, was at last asking him to declare himself? Perhaps. Did he know that his answer would seal his death and, more than that, give a final official stamp to Israel's rejection of God's good news? That seems to be the thrust of Mark's story. That story made it clear that Jesus had been officially condemned "as deserving death" not because the testimony of his accusers was true but because his own confession was true: "I am; and you will see the Son of man sitting at the right hand of Power, and coming with the clouds of heaven" (vs. 62). It was this imperious declaration which had fully merited the charge of blasphemy. He had claimed to be not only David's son but his Lord (12:37), not only Israel's Servant but its ruler, not only God's messenger but his anointed Son. It was by his own choice and his own word that he had brought upon himself this repudiation by God's people. If this were his true anointing, he could not now deny it to God's high priest; if false, then he had been deluded from the beginning, and the high priest's conclusion of blasphemy had been necessary (vs. 64). Thus the trial before the high priest simply published to the world the decision which Jesus had made in the night watch on the Mount of Olives. In his mission to Israel he would endure to the end.

The trial of Peter, which had been going on at the same time, provides a vivid contrast. Jesus had been condemned by his own confession; faced with a less serious charge, Peter was freed by his own denial. Jesus had been innocent of the charges others had shouted; Peter was guilty: he had been "with the Nazarene" (vs. 67). During the time when Jesus had been under interrogation, Peter warmed himself by the fire with the guards. The Lord had remained undaunted by a massive array of official witnesses; Peter was terrified by the curiosity of a waitress. When asked, Jesus had said simply, "I am"; Peter invoked binding oaths to reinforce his thrice-repeated lie: "I do not know this man." It took a shrill-voiced rooster, announcing the dawn, to bring Peter to his senses. The night of the two trials was over. Jesus had watched throughout the night; his top lieutenants had fallen asleep.

Such is the story which Mark had heard from the Apostles, perhaps including Peter himself. Mark recognized that this story was an authentic Christian testimony to Jesus. What made the testimony sound authentic? Was it Mark's confidence that every detail had been verified by an eyewitness? That the proceedings had been accurately recorded by an expert secretary? No. The more impressive clue to its authenticity was the candid picture of the disciples' weakness. Only men who had shared Peter's cowardice could give such overwhelming evidence of the Master's strength under fire.

Innocent or Guilty? (15:1-15)

Ever since the original event, men have found it difficult to apportion blame to the various groups which joined in murdering Jesus. According to all the New Testament accounts, both the Jewish and the Roman leaders were implicated. But in some, the onus falls more heavily on the Romans, in others on the Jews. The tendency of one report to hold the Romans accountable may often have been due to the particular situation of the reporter; to him the most dangerous foes to the Church were the political authorities. The tendency of other reports to blame the Jews often reflects on the part of their writers a different predicament, in which the synagogue leaders were the Church's most implacable opponents. Usually, as was the case in Mark's Rome, the worst crises faced by the Church arose from the co-operation of political and religious foes. Often the synagogues created the public unrest and voiced the charges of sedition; this clamor then attracted the notice of the police. Most situations were of this sort; Jesus' encounter with a twofold opposition, symbolized by the two hearings, was repeated in the Church for many decades.

But to whom did Mark's story assign the preponderance of guilt? A preliminary answer may be found on the surface. It was the "whole council" of Jewish leaders who "led him away and delivered him to Pilate" (vs. 1). It was they who brought the charges, and not Pilate's own agents (vs. 3). Moreover, the response of Jesus to Pilate's query strikes a different note from his answer to the high priest (compare 15:2 and 14:61-62). In the latter case, when questioned by a representative of Israel, Jesus had answered clearly and unequivocally (according to Mark; compare Matt. 26:64; Luke 22:67). When he had been questioned, however, by a Roman politician, in political language, "Are you the King of the Jews?", Jesus had replied, "You have said so." Did Jesus reply in this evasive fashion because he did not recognize an obligation to Rome comparable to his duty to Israel?

Perhaps. Possibly, too, he knew that to affirm this title would only confuse things, because to Pilate it would assert a claim to immediate political authority. In any case, Pilate was unable to establish just grounds for execution. Left alone, Pilate would have let Jesus go. Thus far, Mark appears to acquit the Romans of major guilt.

The next incident seems to corroborate this conclusion. Pilate three times indicated a willingness to release Jesus (vss. 9, 12, 14). He was impelled to ask, "What evil has he done?" (vs. 14). Pilate's desire for justice, however, was weak and short-lived. In spite of his knowledge that "envy" was a factor (vs. 10), he was more intent on satisfying the crowd (vs. 15) than on dispensing justice. Yielding to opportunism, he scourged Jesus and delivered him to be crucified. In telling the story of this trial scene Mark was concerned not so much to free Pilate of the guilt of crucifying Jesus as to show that the action of Jewish authorities had the full support of Israel. It was the crowd of Israelites who preferred the release of a political insurrectionist, a murderer, Barabbas (vs. 11), and who shouted again and again, "Crucify him."

We return to the question of how Mark apportioned the responsibility. The answer, I believe, is twofold: First, no one proved to be without guilt. Everyone had shared in the outcome. Mark agreed with Paul: "All men, both Jews and Greeks, are under the power of sin" (Rom. 3:9); for him as for Paul, this truth had been exhibited in the death of Jesus.

Second, Mark believed that guilt for rejecting Jesus increased in proportion to previous Covenant obligations to God. Because they belonged to the Covenant People, the Jewish crowd (vs. 14) was more culpable than Pilate or his cohorts. More culpable, in turn, than the crowd were the authorized rulers of Israel (vss. 10-11), including Pharisees and Sadducees, scribes, elders, and priests. Still more culpable was Judas, who had willingly agreed to be their tool. Even more guilty than Judas were the disciples who had fled, chief of whom was Peter. In this assignment of guilt, Mark believed he had Peter's own support (14:72). These men Jesus had called and taught. He had shared with them his authority and power. He had revealed to them the mysteries of the Kingdom, warning them repeatedly and countering their fears. With them he had broken bread on that very day. To the question, to whom belongs the shame, then, Mark answers, "All," and more often, "We." He would have agreed heartily with First Peter, in his quotation from Isaiah: "He himself bore our sins in his body on the tree" (I Peter 2:24; Isa. 53:4).

At this point, therefore, we may refer back to our outline of Mark's message. "The good news which Jesus had preached about God" could become "the good news which the Apostles preached about Jesus" only after they had fulfilled Jesus' prophecy of their flight (14:27), and after he had sealed them with the "blood of the covenant . . . poured out for many" (14:24).

The King's Enthronement (15:16-39)

The New Testament is filled with haunting and glorious paradoxes. Of these we have noted a small sampling: the wealth of the poor, the joy of the sorrowing, the power of weakness, the sin of the righteous, the glory disclosed in shame, the foolishness of wisdom. These reversals of ordinary human logic were all grounded in the one event: the life in death of the Son of God. He was executed as "King of the Jews" (vs. 18), yet this was in fact his enthronement as King. In this event, the last truly became first (10:45).

Mark's account of this event is somber and glorious. Perhaps we should read it in the way we listen to great music, like the *Passions* of Bach. We should listen not to the separate words but to the recurring cadences and rhythms. We should sense the contrapuntal movement which weaves together the strident shrieks of the mob and the quiet deep voice of God. To read the story thus may help us to detect the profound ironies beneath the surface. What the scoffers say about their target is true, startlingly true. Yet they are sure that it is false; they are laughing at the joke it would be if it were true. Perhaps, behind the scene, God is holding them in derision. At least that was the conviction of many Christians of Mark's day, who read the account of Good Friday with one eye on Psalm 2. They had told the story often, fusing it with Psalms and prophecies on the one hand (for example, Ps. 22; Isa. 53), and with their own experiences of shame and ridicule on the other. If one reads looking for exact historical data, the text becomes opaque and a mere collection of riddles. But if one reads to observe the irony of the situation (the King of all, being enthroned amid the taunts of all), he will find the music more transparent.

Where does the King go? First of all "inside the palace," led by the whole battalion of soldiers (vs. 16). How inappropriate yet appropriate! The soldiers dress him in the royal robe, and for him they devise a crown (vs. 17). They shout praises to him, give him a royal scepter, and kneel in homage before him (vs. 19). Ribald and vulgar, they revel in their rowdy sport, yet unwittingly this very humiliation is the true mark of his dignity. "By his wounds you have been healed" (I Peter 2:24).

The irony continues en route to Golgotha. No disciple is available to help with the cross, so the soldiers impress a passer-by to carry it. When Mark introduces Simon, he mentions his sons, who possibly had become well-known Christians, thus indicating perhaps how this very cross had been instrumental in converting men. At nine o'clock came the crucifixion and the nakedness. The soldiers took from him his last remaining possession, his clothing, and made sport by gambling for the separate pieces. How telling this picture of shame and poverty! "Though he was rich, yet for your sake he became poor" (II Cor. 8:9). He was lifted aloft as a king, and like any king he needed chief officers, viceregents. So they gave him two robbers, to take the places for which the two disciples had blindly asked (10:35-45). Even these thieves joined in the abuse (vs. 32). Everyone joined in the mockery: soldiers (vs. 19), passers-by (vs. 29), chief priests and scribes (vs. 31), thieves (vs. 32). Had he predicted the Temple's destruction? Let him come down from the cross (vss. 29-30). They did not know that the Temple was being destroyed and rebuilt from that very throne, having no suspicion of the strength of this weakness. "He saved others; he cannot save himself" was meant as a jest, but for Mark it concealed a final truth. Only because Christ did not spare himself was he even then saving others, giving his life as a ransom for those very men (10:45). They called again for signs. What could be more convincing than a descent from the cross "that we may see and believe"? (vs. 32). But to those who believed, this cross became the final sign of God's power and God's wisdom (I Cor. 1:24). By it this King was establishing his authority over "the rulers of this age" (I Cor. 2:8). They thought he was so firmly nailed that he could not come down; they little realized that he was nailing to the cross "the bond which stood against us with its legal demands" (Col. 2:14). Thus through the entire morning, from nine until noon, men of all kinds continued their lampooning, all the while unwittingly giving evidence of God's miraculous grace: "For our sake he made him to be sin who knew no sin" (II Cor. 5:21).

From noon until three p.m. "there was darkness over the whole land" (vs. 33). What kind of darkness was this? Surely Mark knew it represented more than an accidental solar eclipse, more than a cosmic portent. We must look elsewhere in Scripture for hints. Was this the darkness which would not be able to overcome the light (John 1:5), the darkness in which all men walk so long as they do not recognize the light (John 8:12)? Was it that deep darkness which Amos had promised for the Day of the Lord? (Amos 5:18). Perhaps it symbolized the kingdom of death with which Jesus was contending for the souls of those who die. Perhaps it was the shadows in which, as Isaiah knew, all men sit waiting for their redemption (Matt. 4:16; Isa. 9:2). Did Mark mean to accent the darkness in the minds and hearts of the onlookers (Rom. 1:21; 11:10), or that more terrible darkness for Jesus, in which he experienced the withdrawal of God's supporting hands (vs. 34; Ps. 22:1)? The nearest parallel to Mark's thought may appear in Luke where Jesus said to his enemies: "This is your hour, and the power of darkness" (22:53). In this hour of their triumph, when he is utterly under their control, Satan's power has reached its maximum. For Satan was widely considered the ruler of darkness. Here, then, he shows his greatest strength, so that to defeat him now would be a decisive defeat from which he would never recover. And that is what the Man on the cross did. In dying for men, he defeated the world rulers of darkness and delivered men from their clutch (Eph. 6:12; Col. 1:12). With Jesus at the point of death, the scene on Golgotha represented the fullest marshaling of the demonic forces, the most conclusive proof of the weakness of God's emissary, and therefore the place where victory on the part of the King of the Jews would make him in truth King of all kings (Rev. 11:15; 19:16). Mark's story gave two tokens of that victory: the rending of the Temple veil and the startled cry of the centurion.

The veil was the curtain which separated the Holy of Holies from the rest of the Temple. It protected the innermost shrine from contamination by the worshipers. Only the high priest could enter once a year after he had offered sacrifices for his own sins and those of the people. It was that most holy place where God himself in his infinite glory had chosen to bestow his Presence. For this curtain to be torn so that it could never be restored was the symbol of ominous, awesome changes in God's dealings with his people. To early Christians, and we must go to them for explanation, these changes were described in many different ways. Jesus himself had now become the High Priest, entering into the presence of God where he makes intercessions for men. His sacrifice replaced and redefined all other sacrifices. He had atoned for men's sins, giving the one full and perfect sacrifice. His New Covenant had fulfilled the old and had made it obsolete (Heb. 8). His body, broken on the cross, had provided the only access for' men to God, and for God to men. His body had become in fact God's temple, the house where God dwells with his people. The high priest of the one Temple had succeeded in destroying Jesus, but in the tearing of the curtain God had declared his failure. The vineyard would now be given to others (12:9-10).

Similarly, the word of the centurion (vs. 39) demonstrated the failure of the Roman power. The high priests of Israel had delivered the Son of Man to the Gentiles (10:33). He had been delivered over by Pilate to the soldiers (15:15). The soldiers had mocked him and spat upon him. As the head of their execution squad, the centurion had made sure they had done their job. He must stay until he could report to his chief that the mission had been accomplished and that the criminal was dead (vs. 45). He it was who gave the first confession to Jesus' Sonship. His simple words blotted out the taunts and scourgings. He gave his witness to all the ribald lies and unconscious truths which had been uttered. Silently the dying Jesus had preached his gospel to the most hostile congregation, and God had demonstrated the power of the Cross. Even before the burial, that power had done its work over two of the groups present, over the passers-by in the case of Simon of Cyrene and over the Roman troops in the case of this centurion. The sequel will show the promise of new life even to a member of the Sanhedrin (vs. 43) and ultimately to the erstwhile disciples (16:7).

Fear and Trembling (15:40—16:8)

During the King's enthronement, his closest disciples, the Twelve, had been absent. This is worth remarking, because they had been constantly with Jesus since the opening of his crusade. At cockcrow on this dread day the last one had disappeared (14:72). Where were they? Presumably still in flight. Jesus' important word, however, had been only halfway accomplished. This word, uttered after supper on the previous evening, must be recalled: "I will strike the shepherd, and the sheep will be scat-

tered" (14:27). This had been fulfilled. God had struck down the
Shepherd, for Mark knew that God had remained in the shadows
around the scaffold, and that all had happened in accordance with
his will. The sheep had been scattered. Then how were they to be
gathered again? The second half of Jesus' prophecy had given the
answer: "After I am raised up, I will go before you to Galilee"
(14:28). This half had not yet been fulfilled, so the rest of the
narrative tells of its fulfillment (16:7). Mark will not stop writing
before that point.

But let us return to Golgotha. What took place by way of epi-
logue after the centurion's amazing confession?

First, a group of women was introduced. They seem to spring
from nowhere, since Mark has not mentioned them earlier—a
striking reminder of how much his story omits. They were neither
unknown nor unimportant. In Galilee they had followed Jesus and
ministered to him (vs. 41). They had been close enough to his
party to join the pilgrimage to Jerusalem. Perhaps they had lifted
their voices at the Triumphal Entry (11:9). Whatever they had
done, Mark had displayed little interest in them (which fact does
not make him an antifeminist). He needs them now, however, to
show how Jesus fulfilled his promise to the Twelve.

The women had watched from afar the long hours of mockery
and agony. They had seen Jesus die. Testimonies to the actual dying later became important to Christians in meeting Jewish attacks
and in resisting Gnostic heresies. Not only Pilate (vss. 44-45) but
also the centurion and the women could vouch for the reality of
his death. More important still, they watched "where he was laid"
(vs. 47).

The account of the burial requires little comment. It was Jewish law that a corpse must not be allowed to remain over the Sabbath uninterred. After the last loud cry (vs. 37), little time was
left before sundown. Hurriedly a member of the Sanhedrin, which
had condemned Jesus, secured an official permit to bury him. This
took "courage," not only to risk Pilate's suspicions but to risk the
hatred of his colleagues on the Council. It also required more than
courage. For a family's burial chambers to be used for the corpse
of an executed criminal was bound to pollute those chambers. Joseph's motives must have been very strong for him to do this, but
the only explanation Mark gives is this: Joseph "was also himself
looking for the kingdom of God." This characterization may remind us of the scribe who was not far from the Kingdom

(12:34), and of the rich man whose only sorrow was unwillingness to sell all (10:21-22). In telling the story, however, Mark
was interested in the links between the tomb, the women, and the
Twelve (vs. 47).

Late on Friday afternoon, Joseph had completed his sad duty.
Early on Sunday morning, some thirty-six hours later, the women
came to do theirs. The body had yet to be anointed, a task for
which there had been no time on Friday, and such work was forbidden on the Sabbath. On arrival they discovered that Jesus had
received a higher anointing. Or rather, in less metaphorical language, they were amazed by two things. The huge round stone
which had been used as a door into the burial cave had been
rolled back. Entering the tomb, they saw, sitting on the ledge
where they expected to find the corpse, a heavenly messenger. The
"white robe" of the "young man" almost surely indicates that he
is serving as an angel to bring a word from God to them. They,
and the readers as well, realize that this word is of first importance. Verse 6 gives part of the message: "He has risen, he is not
here." This word, of course, had many overtones for Mark's
readers. Amazement is natural, but it is quietly rebuked. Those
who seek for Jesus in a tomb will not find him there. The shelf
where Joseph had laid his body is empty. The message from God
is itself assumed to be sufficient for faith. This laconic announcement (like that with which Jesus had begun his work, 1:15) answers very few questions of the skeptical or pious. When did he
arise? By what means? In what form? By what evidence may we
be sure? No such questions are answered. Rather is a single truth
announced: "He has risen." All else seems nonessential.

Mark shows greater interest, however, in the message of verse
7. Here there is a command, "Go." God does not disclose the Resurrection fact except to enlist people in a task. The women must
go to the Twelve with a special message; not a new one, to be
sure (14:28), but a most important one. They must tell his disciples and Peter: "He is going before you to Galilee; there you will
see him." Did the disciples understand the full import? Many
readers, at least, do not. Questions galore spring to our minds, especially if we compare the Marcan account with the other Gospels. All the problems concerning the Resurrection intrude, but
here we must be content with Mark's words. At the very least,
they underscore the assurance that both the Most High God and
the most lowly Son were deeply concerned about the disciples,

and especially about Peter (distinguished here perhaps in the same way and for the same reason he was distinguished at the Last Supper; see 14:29-31). They were supremely concerned about the disciples' return to Galilee and their work there. The movements of the disciples were now to be determined by Jesus' promise that he would go before them, just as he had gone before them since calling them in Galilee. They have been followers; they will remain followers. "There you will see him, as he told you." Does this refer to such an encounter as is described in John 21 or Matthew 28? Or does it refer to the climactic vision of their Lord after they have endured, like Stephen, to the end? (Acts 7:55-56). Or does it refer to seeing the Son of Man coming at the close of the age? (Mark 13:26). Perhaps one, perhaps all three. In any case, a sequel is expected, a necessary sequel. Nor does Mark tell us what it is. He insists, however, that this story is incomplete without a later development; and the later development will be unintelligible without this story as its beginning. The women carry the message of Resurrection to the Twelve, who will then carry the message of Resurrection to the world, "beginning from Galilee after the baptism which John preached" (Acts 10:37-43). The story of Jesus' baptism will be the beginning of their message; the Presence of the Risen Lord will be the source of their power and the goal of their endurance. It is in such a direction that God's message to the women points.

And now we come to the last verse, perhaps the most difficult of all, and certainly a strange way for even a strange book to end: "for they were afraid." In the Greek the sentence seems to break off in the middle, as if the thought had not been completed. So strange was this ending that many early scribes filled in what they thought was lacking, and some of their additions still remain in the manuscripts. They compared Mark with the other Gospels (which of course were written one to three decades later than Mark) and became convinced that Mark must have intended to include similar stories of how Jesus had been seen by his disciples. Scholars are in agreement that these stories (16:9-19) do not come from the book Mark wrote. They are not in agreement on whether Mark intended to stop at 16:8. It is possible that a column or two from his scroll was accidentally torn off, or that it became tattered from frequent use. It is even possible that some editor tore it off because he did not like what it contained. But whatever explanation is adopted for this abrupt ending, we must be content to expound the text as it stands. The writer of this commentary believes that Mark fully intended to halt his account with this verse.

The chief impact of the verse is simply to describe the indescribable. The key words all show this. The amazement of the women (vs. 5) turns into trembling, astonishment, fear, flight, silence. All of these are considered in the Bible to be appropriate and normal human responses to an appearance of God, to a message from God, to an event in which God's power is released. The prophets all knew this fear and trembling (for example, Isa. 6). They all knew the unutterable weakness of those who receive God's call. Fear stresses the reality of the divine power and glory. Flight (very different from the flight at Jesus' arrest) accents the unbearable character of the presence of God. Silence is appropriate to God's speaking, and to the stupendous impact of God's word. Who can stand when he appears? Who can speak when he speaks? Who can remain calm when he gives a commission? At least the women could not, and presumably neither could the disciples when the message from the women had been delivered, starting them on their new work.